in honor of

Marc Clearfield

THE
CIVIL WAR
A NATION DIVIDED

Women
and the Civil War

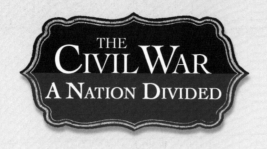

THE CIVIL WAR
A NATION DIVIDED

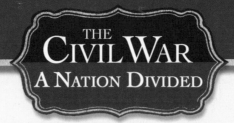

THE
CIVIL WAR
A NATION DIVIDED

Women
and the Civil War

Louise Chipley Slavicek

CHELSEA HOUSE
PUBLISHERS
An imprint of Infobase Publishing

WOMEN AND THE CIVIL WAR

Chelsea House
An imprint of Infobase Publishing
132 West 31st Street
New York NY 10001

Library of Congress Cataloging-in-Publication Data
Slavicek, Louise Chipley, 1956–
  Women and the Civil War / by Louise Chipley Slavicek.
    p. cm. — (The Civil War : a nation divided)
  Includes bibliographical references and index.
  ISBN 978-1-60413-040-9 (hardcover)
  1. United States—History—Civil War, 1861–1865—Women. 2. United States—History—Civil War, 1861–1865—Participation, Female. 3. Women—United States—History—19th century. 4. Women—Confederate States of America. I. Title.

  E628.S63 2009
  973.7082—dc22   2008026562

Chelsea House books are available at special discounts when purchased in bulk quantities for businesses, associations, institutions, or sales promotions. Please call our Special Sales Department in New York at (212) 967-8800 or (800) 322-8755.

You can find Chelsea House on the World Wide Web at
http://www.chelseahouse.com

Series design by Lina Farinella
Cover design by Takeshi Takahashi

Printed in the United States of America

Bang NMSG 10 9 8 7 6 5 4 3 2 1

This book is printed on acid-free paper.

All links and Web addresses were checked and verified to be correct at the time of publication. Because of the dynamic nature of the Web, some addresses and links may have changed since publication and may no longer be valid.

Contents

Chronology

1820 The Missouri Compromise allows Maine to be admitted to the Union as a free state and Missouri as a slave state in 1821.

1831 William Lloyd Garrison publishes the first issue of his abolitionist newspaper, *The Liberator*.

1836 The House of Representatives passes a gag rule that automatically tables or postpones action on all petitions relating to slavery without hearing them.

1838 The Underground Railroad is formally organized.

1845 Former slave Frederick Douglass publishes his autobiography, *Narrative of the Life of Frederick Douglass, An American Slave*.

1850 Congress enacts several measures that together make up the Compromise of 1850.

1852 Harriet Beecher Stowe publishes *Uncle Tom's Cabin*.

1854 Congress passes the Kansas-Nebraska Act, which overturns the Missouri Compromise and thus opens northern territories to slavery.

1855 As Kansas prepares to vote, thousands of Border Ruffians from Missouri enter the territory in an attempt to influence the elections. This begins the period known as Bleeding Kansas.

1856 South Carolina representative Preston Brooks attacks Massachusetts senator Charles Sumner on the Senate floor and beats him with a cane.

1857   The Supreme Court rules, in *Dred Scott v. Sandford*, that blacks are not U.S. citizens and slaveholders have the right to take slaves into free areas of the country.

1859   John Brown seizes the arsenal at Harpers Ferry, Virginia. Robert E. Lee, then a Federal Army regular, leads the troops that capture Brown.

1860   **NOVEMBER**   Abraham Lincoln is elected president.

DECEMBER   A South Carolina convention passes an ordinance of secession, and the state secedes from the Union.

1861   **JANUARY**   Florida, Alabama, Georgia, and Louisiana secede from the Union.

FEBRUARY   Texas votes to secede from the Union. The Confederate States of America is formed and elects Jefferson Davis as its president.

MARCH   Abraham Lincoln is sworn in as the sixteenth president of the United States and delivers his first inaugural address.

APRIL 12   At 4:30 A.M., Confederate forces fire on South Carolina's Fort Sumter. The Civil War begins. Virginia secedes from the Union five days later.

MAY   Arkansas and North Carolina secede from the Union.

JUNE   Tennessee secedes from the Union.

JULY 21   The Union suffers a defeat in northern Virginia, at the First Battle of Bull Run (Manassas).

AUGUST   The Confederates win the Battle of Wilson's Creek, in Missouri.

1862   **FEBRUARY 6**   In Tennessee, Union general Ulysses S. Grant captures Fort Henry. Ten days later, he captures Fort Donelson.

MARCH The Confederate ironclad ship CSS *Virginia* (formerly the USS *Merrimack*) battles the Union ironclad *Monitor* to a draw. The Union's Peninsular Campaign begins in Virginia.

APRIL 6–7 Ulysses S. Grant defeats Confederate forces in the Battle of Shiloh (Pittsburg Landing), in Tennessee.

APRIL 24 David Farragut moves his fleet of Union Navy vessels up the Mississippi River to take New Orleans.

MAY 31 The Battle of Seven Pines (Fair Oaks) takes place in Virginia.

JUNE 1 Robert E. Lee assumes command of the Army of Northern Virginia.

JUNE 25–JULY 1 The Seven Days Battles are fought in Virginia.

AUGUST 29–30 The Union is defeated at the Second Battle of Bull Run.

SEPTEMBER 17 The bloodiest day in U.S. military history: Confederate forces under Robert E. Lee are stopped at Antietam, Maryland, by Union forces under George B. McClellan.

SEPTEMBER 22 The first Emancipation Proclamation to free slaves in the rebellious states is issued by President Lincoln.

DECEMBER 13 The Union's Army of the Potomac, under Ambrose Burnside, suffers a costly defeat at Fredericksburg, Virginia.

1863 **JANUARY 1** President Lincoln issues the final Emancipation Proclamation.

JANUARY 29 Ulysses S. Grant is placed in command of the Army of the West, with orders to capture Vicksburg, Mississippi.

MAY 1–4   Union forces under Joseph Hooker are defeated decisively by Robert E. Lee's much smaller forces at the Battle of Chancellorsville, in Virginia.

MAY 10   The South suffers a huge blow as General Thomas "Stonewall" Jackson dies from wounds he received during the battle of Chancellorsville.

JUNE 3   Robert E. Lee launches his second invasion of the North; he heads into Pennsylvania with 75,000 Confederate troops.

JULY 1–3   The tide of war turns against the South as the Confederates are defeated at the Battle of Gettysburg in Pennsylvania.

JULY 4   Vicksburg, the last Confederate stronghold on the Mississippi River, surrenders to Ulysses S. Grant after a six-week siege.

JULY 13–16   Antidraft riots rip through New York City.

JULY 18   The black 54th Massachusetts Infantry Regiment under Colonel Robert Gould Shaw assaults a fortified Confederate position at Fort Wagner, South Carolina.

SEPTEMBER 19–20   A decisive Confederate victory takes place at Chickamauga, Tennessee.

NOVEMBER 19   President Lincoln delivers the Gettysburg Address.

NOVEMBER 23–25   Ulysses S. Grant's Union forces win an important victory at the Battle of Chattanooga, in Tennessee.

1864   **MARCH 9**   President Lincoln names Ulysses S. Grant general-in-chief of all the armies of the United States.

MAY 4   Ulysses S. Grant opens a massive, coordinated campaign against Robert E. Lee's Confederate armies in Virginia.

MAY 5–6   The Battle of the Wilderness is fought in Virginia.

MAY 8–12   The Battle of Spotsylvania is fought in Virginia.

JUNE 1–3   The Battle of Cold Harbor is fought in Virginia.

JUNE 15   Union forces miss an opportunity to capture Petersburg, Virginia; this results in a nine-month Union siege of the city.

SEPTEMBER 2   Atlanta, Georgia, is captured by Union forces led by William Tecumseh Sherman.

OCTOBER 19   Union general Philip H. Sheridan wins a decisive victory over Confederate general Jubal Early in the Shenandoah Valley of Virginia.

NOVEMBER 8   Abraham Lincoln is reelected president, defeating Democratic challenger George B. McClellan.

NOVEMBER 15   General William T. Sherman begins his March to the Sea from Atlanta.

DECEMBER 15–16   Confederate general John Bell Hood is defeated at Nashville, Tennessee, by Union forces under George H. Thomas.

DECEMBER 21   General Sherman reaches Savannah, Georgia; he leaves behind a path of destruction 300 miles long and 60 miles wide from Atlanta to the sea.

1865   Southern states begin to pass Black Codes.

JANUARY 31   The U.S. Congress approves the Thirteenth Amendment to the United States Constitution.

FEBRUARY 3   A peace conference takes place as President Lincoln meets with Confederate Vice President Alexander Stephens at Hampton Roads, Virginia; the meeting ends in failure, and the war continues.

MARCH 4   Lincoln delivers his second inaugural address ("With Malice Toward None"). Congress establishes the Freedmen's Bureau.

MARCH 25   Robert E. Lee's Army of Northern Virginia begins its last offensive with an attack on the center of

Ulysses S. Grant's forces at Petersburg, Virginia. Four hours later, Lee's attack is broken.

APRIL 2   Grant's forces begin a general advance and break through Lee's lines at Petersburg. Lee evacuates Petersburg. Richmond, Virginia, the Confederate capital, is evacuated.

APRIL 9   Robert E. Lee surrenders his Confederate Army to Ulysses S. Grant at the village of Appomattox Court House, Virginia.

APRIL 14   John Wilkes Booth shoots President Lincoln at Ford's Theatre in Washington, D.C.

APRIL 15   President Abraham Lincoln dies. Vice President Andrew Johnson assumes the presidency.

APRIL 18   Confederate general Joseph E. Johnston surrenders to Union general William T. Sherman in North Carolina.

APRIL 26   John Wilkes Booth is shot and killed in a tobacco barn in Virginia.

DECEMBER   The Thirteenth Amendment is ratified.

1866   Congress approves the Fourteenth Amendment to the Constitution.

Congress passes the Civil Rights Act.

The responsibilities and powers of the Freedmen's Bureau are expanded by Congress. The legislation is vetoed by President Johnson, but Congress overrides his veto.

The Ku Klux Klan is established in Tennessee.

1867   Congress passes the Military Reconstruction Act.

Congress passes the Tenure of Office Act.

1868   The impeachment trial of President Andrew Johnson ends in acquittal.

Ulysses S. Grant is elected president.

1869   Congress approves the Fifteenth Amendment to the Constitution.

1871   The Ku Klux Klan Act is passed by Congress.

1872   President Grant is reelected.

1875   A new Civil Rights Act is passed.

1877   Rutherford B. Hayes assumes the presidency.
        The Reconstruction Era ends.

American Women Confront the Civil War

"You mustn't trouble you[r] Self about me," Sarah Rosetta Wakeman wrote to her parents on March 29, 1863, from Virginia, where she was serving with the Union Army under the male alias Lyons Wakeman. "I don't fear the rebel bullets nor I don't fear the cannon," the 20-year-old assured her family back home in the small town of Afton, New York. Once widely considered "the weaker sex," emotionally as well as physically, women were officially barred from serving in the Union and Confederate armies during the Civil War. But Rosetta Wakeman, who stood just 5 feet tall (1.5 meters), took great pride in the fact that she could drill and handle a rifle with as much skill as any man in her regiment. "It would make your hair stand out to be where I have been. How would you like to be in the front rank and have the rear load and fire their guns over your shoulder? I have been there my Self," Wakeman informed her parents, with obvious satisfaction.

During the spring of 1864, Wakeman was in Louisiana as part of the North's Red River Campaign. The young farmwoman, who had dared to ignore custom and military regulations to fight for her country, took pride in her stamina and courage as a soldier. "I have marched two hundred miles," she boasted in a letter home: "We was ten days on the road amarching." On April 9, Wakeman helped her regiment successfully drive back six charges by Confederate troops at Pleasant Hill near Shreveport, Louisiana. "I was under fire for four hours and laid on the field of battle all night," she reported to her parents a few days later.

The following June, Wakeman's illegal two-year stint in the army came to a tragic end when she lost a battle with dysentery at the age of 21. Inscribed on her simple gravestone in Louisiana's Chalmette National Cemetery is the name "Lyons Wakeman." Wakeman had managed to keep the secret of her gender from the army to the very end. It was only when her letters home surfaced nearly a century after her death that the U.S. government discovered Private Wakeman's true identity.

THE DEADLIEST WAR IN U.S. HISTORY

In April 1861 the American people—male and female—embarked upon what was to be the deadliest war in their nation's history: the Civil War. In all, more than 600,000 soldiers perished during the four-year-long war; two-thirds of them, including Private "Lyons" Wakeman, died from disease rather than from battlefield injuries. More than a century and a half after the war, historians are still debating the various causes of the devastating conflict—economic, political, social, and cultural. Yet most agree that at the very heart of the struggle was the enslavement of African Americans, the South's so-called "peculiar institution."

By the middle of the nineteenth century, slavery had been outlawed in all the Northern states but still was flourishing in the South. Some 4 million African-American slaves lived

During the Civil War, women contributed time, labor, and money to help support the soldiers. By working outside the home as nurses, factory hands, and domestic laborers, women provided vital assistance to both the Union and the Confederacy. Above, female nurses and officers of the U.S. Sanitation Commission, a Civil War volunteer group.

and toiled there, the majority of them on the region's vast cotton plantations. During the presidential campaign of 1860, Republican candidate Abraham Lincoln of Illinois had called for an end to the expansion of slavery within U.S. territory, although he promised not to interfere with slavery in those states where human bondage already was established. When the results of the November election were tallied, it was discovered that Lincoln had carried every Northern state except for one and not a single Southern state. The war that erupted between North and South just five months after the election was sparked by Southern suspicions that, despite his campaign pledge, Lincoln intended to abolish slavery throughout the United States. It was a move many white Southerners believed would destroy their cotton-based economy and entire way of life.

By the time of Lincoln's inauguration on March 4, 1861, seven Southern states—South Carolina, Florida, Mississippi, Georgia, Louisiana, Alabama, and Texas—already had seceded, or withdrawn, from the Union. They declared themselves the independent Confederate States of America, with Mississippi politician Jefferson Davis as their president. On April 12 of that year, South Carolina militiamen seized the Union's Fort Sumter in Charleston.

Absolutely committed to restoring the fractured Union, Lincoln asked the states to provide 75,000 volunteers to put down what he referred to as the Confederate "insurrection," or rebellion. Lincoln's call to arms was greeted enthusiastically in the North, but in the South it caused four more states—Arkansas, Tennessee, North Carolina, and Virginia—to sever all ties with the federal government and join the Confederacy. The Civil War had officially begun, and Northerners and Southerners alike confidently assumed that the struggle would be brief and glorious. In April 1861, few could have dreamed that by the time the war finally ended four long years later, it would have caused more than a million deaths and injuries and touched the lives of virtually every man, woman, and child in the nation.

NEW CHALLENGES AND NEW ROLES

Women were officially banned from combat duty by the Union and Confederate governments. Nevertheless, they played a vital role in both the Northern and Southern war efforts. Between 1861 and 1865, women donated hundreds of thousands of dollars worth of desperately needed supplies to the Union and Confederate armies. Women also nursed and comforted ill and wounded soldiers and helped produce ammunition and other military materials in government weapons stores. They kept plantations, farms, and businesses running while their male relations were off fighting. Determined to confront the enemy face-to-face on the battlefield, some like Rosetta Wakeman even went so far as to disguise themselves as men and enlist in their nation's armed forces. Others risked their lives as spies, scouts, messengers, or saboteurs to further their side's cause.

By participating in these various wartime activities—charitable, medical, economic, and military—hundreds of thousands of women in the North and South were taking on tasks and responsibilities that were completely new and unfamiliar to them. At the same time, these new experiences were pushing many American women well beyond the boundaries of what had long been viewed as a female's proper place: the private world of home and family.

In the United States and throughout the Western world during the nineteenth century, most people—male and female alike—considered a woman's place to be in the home. Financial need forced many lower-class American women to become wage earners, usually as maids or other servants. Yet it was highly unusual for middle- or upper-class women to work outside their homes before the Civil War. Closed out of virtually all professions except teaching, women also were barred from voting or holding political office. They were supposed to be submissive, retiring, devout, and interested only in childcare, housekeeping, and other domestic matters. Those who attempted to break out

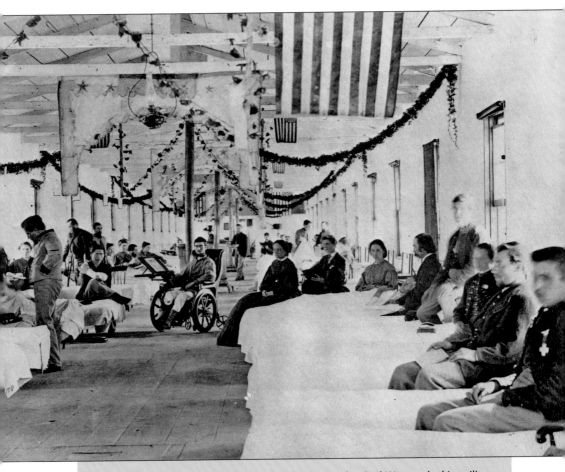

Many of the women who served as nurses during the Civil War worked in military hospitals, tending ill and wounded soldiers (above). In addition to working long shifts that did not allow them any time to eat or rest, women had to endure sexism from male staff members as well as the emotional toll of comforting the crippled and the dying.

of these restrictive roles typically were scorned as unladylike and immodest.

Between 1861 and 1865, however, patriotism and concern for loved ones, friends, and neighbors in the armed forces inspired large numbers of American women to challenge traditional ideas of what was "female" behavior. Many ventured beyond their usual domestic sphere to volunteer for soldier relief and other war-related activities. Other women sought paid work outside the customary haven of home and hearth when male breadwinners marched off to war.

During the war, women of all races and social classes gained a new sense of independence and confidence by taking part in civic and economic activities that previously had been considered off-limits for the supposedly "weaker sex." Yet at the same time, the war brought enormous hardship and tragedy to the country's female population. The most lethal struggle in U.S. history was a period of tremendous uncertainty and loss for countless American women. This was particularly true in the South, where a higher proportion of the male population fought and died in the war, and where food shortages, skyrocketing prices, and repeated enemy invasions caused widespread anxiety and suffering. In confronting the heavy emotional, economic, and physical challenges that the Civil War created, American women showed courage and rescourcefulness. They demonstrated that even though they were officially forbidden from joining their male compatriots on the battlefield, they were fighters nonetheless.

Caring for the
Wounded and Sick

When the Civil War began in April 1861, few Americans could have imagined the bloodshed and physical suffering that the conflict would bring. Over the course of four long years of fighting, some 620,000 soldiers perished—an average of more than 400 deaths per day. At least 500,000 additional troops suffered battlefield wounds, many of them severe enough to cause lifelong disabilities.

Throughout the war, women on both sides of the struggle played a vital role in caring for the huge numbers of injured and ill. Thousands of female nurses were assigned to general military facilities or hospital transport ships well-removed from the fighting. Others tended to the wounded at makeshift field hospitals near the battlefronts. During the war, more than 20,000 American women—young and old, married and single, wealthy and poor, paid and unpaid—took part in the grueling and often dangerous tasks of healing and comforting legions of wounded and sick soldiers.

WOMEN AND THE UNION ARMY'S HEALTHCARE CRISIS

On the eve of the bloodiest war in U.S. history, there were no general army hospitals anywhere in the United States. Instead, each of the nation's widely scattered army posts supported its

Mary Edwards Walker: The Union Army's First and Only Female Surgeon

In 1861, only a tiny handful of American women held medical degrees. Among this elite group was an ambitious and independent 28-year-old from Upstate New York named Mary Edwards Walker. Edwards had graduated from Syracuse Medical College in 1855, just six years after another New York resident, Englishwoman Elizabeth Blackwell, graduated from Geneva Medical College and became the first female physician in the United States. Walker began her own medical practice in Ohio and later in New York, but she failed to attract many patients in either state. It appeared that most nineteenth-century Americans were not yet ready to accept a woman physician.

Blackwell decided to remain in New York to train military nurses after the Confederate assault on Fort Sumter in April 1861. Walker, on the other hand, immediately headed for Washington, D.C., after the attack to offer her services to the U.S. Army as a physician. At first the Union authorities, unused to the idea of female physicians, refused even to consider Walker's application.

Walker then volunteered as a nurse for several months at military hospitals in Washington, D.C., and took additional medical courses back home in New York. Then, she finally was sent to Tennessee to serve as the Union Army's first—and only—female surgeon. As an assistant surgeon with the Army of the Cumberland, Walker struggled unsuccessfully to win acceptance from her male colleagues. She also received about $30 less per month in wages than the army's other assistant surgeons.

own small hospital. The largest had just 40 beds. They also were woefully understaffed: At the beginning of April 1861, the entire U.S. Army Medical Department consisted of 1 surgeon general, 30 surgeons, 83 assistant surgeons, and not a single nurse

In April 1864, Walker was captured by a Confederate patrol on suspicion of spying when she ventured beyond Union lines. After suffering for four months in a Confederate prison in Richmond, she finally was released as part of an exchange for the Union's release of Confederate prisoners. Walker spent the remainder of the war serving as a physician at a Kentucky women's prison and a Tennessee orphanage.

In recognition of her wartime service, in January 1866 President Andrew Johnson awarded Walker the Congressional Medal of Honor. After the war, instead of trying to revive her small New York medical practice, Walker started traveling and giving lectures. She captured the imagination of audiences all over the country with accounts of her experiences as an army physician and prisoner of war. She also campaigned for women's rights and reform to the cultural rules of female dress. Convinced that traditional female fashions were not only impractical but also unhealthy, Walker, who always wore trousers herself, strongly urged every American woman to adopt male attire.

In 1917, when Walker was 85 years old, Congress voted to take back her Medal of Honor, along with the medals of more than 900 other recipients, after deciding to restrict the honor to those who performed their heroic wartime deeds under enemy fire. Walker refused to return the actual medal, however, and defiantly wore it in public right up until her death two years later. In 1977, the U.S. Army officially returned Walker's Medal of Honor, the only such medal ever awarded to a woman. The army praised her "distinguished gallantry, self-sacrifice, patriotism, dedication, and unflinching loyalty to her country, despite the apparent discrimination because of her sex."

for a force of 16,000 soldiers. Without a permanent nurse corps, the army had to rely on ordinary enlisted men—generally soldiers in recovery from an illness or injury—to nurse their sick comrades. These nurse-soldiers were completely untrained, but they were given hospital work for the sole reason that they were not yet strong enough for their regular duties.

Following the outbreak between North and South at Fort Sumter, South Carolina, on April 12, 1861, many Northerners became concerned about the U.S. Army's ability to meet the medical needs of its troops. Already miniscule, the Army Medical Department's surgical staff was made even smaller when 24 physicians resigned to join the Confederates. The department's lack of a nursing corps was just as worrisome. Union supporters across the North agreed that something had to be done—and quickly—to bolster their army's inadequate medical resources. What it had was clearly not enough.

From the beginning, Union women took a strong interest in the military's healthcare crisis. Barred from serving in combat themselves, Northern women were eager to find other ways to further the Union cause. In April 1861, few issues seemed more urgent than promoting the health and healing of the federal troops. Less than two weeks after the Confederate attack on Fort Sumter, a group of prominent Northern women gathered in New York City to discuss the army's medical emergency. Under the direction of Elizabeth Blackwell, the first woman to be awarded a medical degree in the United States, the group decided to form a national, all-female, humanitarian organization: the Women's Central Association of Relief for the Sick and Wounded of the Army (WCAR). Their mission was twofold: WCAR volunteers would coordinate the distribution of supplies for injured or sick soldiers donated from smaller relief groups, and they also would recruit and train woman nurses to staff the new army hospitals that were sure to open in the months ahead.

Northern women who were eager to participate in the war effort but could not fight on the front lines found other ways to contribute to the Union. Elizabeth Blackwell, above, the first woman in the United States to earn a medical degree, helped coordinate relief efforts by creating the Women's Central Association of Relief for the Sick and Wounded of the Army, a precursor to the U.S. Sanitation Commission.

By summer 1861, WCAR had been absorbed into an even larger national relief organization officially approved by the Department of War and President Lincoln: the United States Sanitary Commission (USSC). Like WCAR, USSC's chief purpose was promoting the physical well-being of the troops. Although the commission's top administrators were men, women took leading roles in all the USSC's various humanitarian activities. These included raising funds to purchase medical supplies and other necessities for wounded and ill troops; sorting and distributing donated items for soldiers from across the country; improving hygiene conditions in army camps; and, last but not least, enlisting female nurses to staff army hospitals.

A FEMALE NURSE CORPS

In June 1861, the same month that USSC won the Lincoln administration's official backing, the campaign to staff military hospitals with female nurses received another major boost: The Department of War appointed Dorothea Dix as the U.S. Army's first superintendent of woman nurses.

Dix, 59 years old, was widely known as a champion of better treatment for prisoners and the mentally ill. She had first volunteered to organize a female nurse corps within days of the attack on Fort Sumter on April 12. Despite the Union Army's critical nursing shortage, however, it took nearly two months for the Department of War to accept Dix's offer. It took another two months after that for Congress to approve legislation authorizing the employment of female nurses in military hospitals.

There were probably several causes for the army's and federal government's hesitancy to create a formal nurse corps during the first months of the conflict. One reason was that many military and civilian officials still clung to the belief that the larger Union forces would rapidly crush their Southern opponents, thereby keeping Northern casualty rates low.

Another reason had to do with popular attitudes toward nursing. At the time that the Civil War erupted, few Americans viewed nursing as a genuine profession. This was not always the case elsewhere in the world. During the Crimean War of the mid-1850s, which pitted Great Britain and its allies against Russia, English nursing pioneer Florence Nightingale organized a highly skilled female nurse corps to care for the British wounded. In doing so, Nightingale helped win professional status for nursing in Europe.

Yet on the other side of the Atlantic Ocean, the idea of nursing as a real profession was slow to take root. Before the Civil War, nursing in the United States still was considered to be the job of a patient's female family members or servants, rather than the job of trained professionals. Indeed, hardly any Americans received nursing care outside of their own homes. The tiny number of civilian hospitals that existed in the United States before the war were charitable institutions staffed largely by Catholic nuns, and they were meant to serve the nation's poorest citizens.

Perhaps the single biggest reason for the army's and Department of War's reluctance to authorize a female nurse corps, however, was the commonly held belief that a military hospital was no place for a woman, especially in wartime. Wartime nursing was a dirty, exhausting, and potentially hazardous job for which "delicate" females were supposedly ill-suited. It was argued that the physical and emotional demands of caring for large numbers of seriously wounded or sick soldiers would be too hard for the so-called weaker sex to bear.

Many Americans also believed it was highly inappropriate for "respectable" women to have intimate contact with the bodies of male soldiers through such duties as dressing wounds or giving sponge baths. Yet nursing involves these sorts of tasks on a regular basis. "No one denied that most women had an aptitude for nursing, that many had gained experience from tending their families and friends," writes Mary Elizabeth Massey

Because of the grim realities of the warfront, many Americans believed that military settings were unsuitable places for women. Some officials believed women were too fragile to work in the harsh conditions of military and field hospitals (above), which could expose them to distressing or dangerous situations.

in *Women in the Civil War*. "Yet public opinion doubted the propriety of their nursing in army hospitals. Refined, modest ladies, said the critics, had no business caring for strange men and certainly not rough, crude soldiers from all walks of life. They would be exposing themselves to embarrassing situations, and the mere thought of what could happen was appalling."

DOROTHEA DIX, SUPERINTENDENT OF WOMAN NURSES

Dorothea Dix was well aware of the popular bias against females working in military hospitals. Therefore, once her appointment became official in June 1861, Dix compiled a long list of strict standards for female hospital applicants. The list clearly was meant to reassure officials and the public about the physical, mental, and moral qualifications of the new nurse corps.

No formal training programs for nurses existed in the United States at the time. Because of this, Dix did not require her appointees to possess any specific medical knowledge or skills beyond what they may have picked up by nursing sick relatives. She did, however, require them to be physically strong, hardworking, and serious-minded:

> Only women of strong health, not subjects of chronic disease, nor liable to sudden illnesses, need apply. . . . [H]abits of neatness, order, sobriety, and industry, are prerequisites. All applicants must present certificates of . . . good character, from at least two persons of trust, testifying to morality, integrity, seriousness, and capacity for care of the sick. . . .

In light of popular concerns regarding contact between female nurses and male soldiers, Dix realized that her appointees would be scrutinized for even the slightest hint of inappropriate behavior. Those hoping to discredit the army's bold experiment in female nursing would be particularly critical. To check this scrutiny before it began, Dix also dictated that all army nurses be at least 30 years of age and "plain" in appearance: "Their dresses," she wrote, "must be brown or black, with no bows, no curls, no jewelry, and no hoops." (Hoops were considered the height of fashion during the 1850s and the first years of the Civil War. These were lightweight, circular frames of cloth-covered steel used to expand a woman's skirt. The idea was that very full skirts made a woman's waist appear smaller.)

Even with Dix's strict selection requirements, her office soon was swamped with applications. In the end, Dix hired 3,000 women to labor in military hospitals in the Washington, D.C., area and elsewhere in the North for the modest wage of 40 cents a day and a ration (a fixed portion of food given to people in military service). By the war's end in 1865, more than 15,000 additional women had nursed in Union hospitals, including some women whom Dix had personally rejected as too young or too glamorous for the job. Many of these nurses received their appointments from one of the North's two largest soldier relief organizations: the U.S. Sanitary Commission, which ran the military's numerous hospital transport ships, and the U.S. Christian Commission, an outgrowth of the YMCA (Young Men's Christian Association). From late 1863 onward, as Union casualties mounted, thousands of women also were hired directly by the chief medical officers of the North's growing number of military hospitals.

FEMALE NURSES IN THE CONFEDERACY

The Confederate Congress did not officially approve the employment of female nurses in army hospitals until the autumn of 1862. Nonetheless, from the war's beginning, Southern women toiled as nurses in both state-run and privately supported hospitals. One example was the Richmond hospital that Virginia heiress Sally Tompkins generously funded in July 1861.

Upper- and middle-class Confederate women were less likely to work in military hospitals than their Union counterparts. Many historians link this fact to the especially rigid standards of social and moral conduct by which Southern women were expected to live. Even more than Northern ideas of what was normal for women, ideals of Southern womanhood stressed the importance of modesty, delicacy, and yielding to

An admirer of the European battlefield nurse Florence Nightingale, Dorothea Dix (above) went to Washington, D.C., to help the Union during the Civil War. Dix set high standards for her nurses and instituted strict rules regarding dress. Dedicated and independent, Dix served as superintendent of female nurses throughout the war without pay.

the authority of husbands or male relatives. Southern novelist Augusta Jane Evans Wilson, for one, expressed exactly this idea to a friend of hers. Wilson wrote that, although she knew the need for nurses was great, her brothers' strong objections led her to feel that she could not work in a Confederate hospital:

"I feel unwilling to take a step which my brothers *disapprove* so vehemently. . . . The boys have heard so much said about ladies being in the hospitals, that they cannot bear for me to go."

Many of the upper- and middle-class Confederate women who did choose to work as nurses clearly felt forced to defend their decisions to their fellow Southerners. Charleston socialite Phoebe Yates Pember was one of these women. In *A Southern Woman's Story*, Pember's account of her wartime service at Richmond's Chimborazo Hospital, she declared:

> There is one subject connected with hospitals on which a few words should be said—the distasteful one that a woman must lose a certain amount of delicacy and reticence in filling any office in them. How can this be? There is no unpleasant exposure under proper arrangements, and even if there be, the circumstances which surround a wounded man, far from friends and home, suffering in a holy cause and dependent upon a woman for help, care and sympathy, hallow and clear the atmosphere in which she labors. . . . A woman *must* soar beyond the conventional modesty considered correct under different circumstances.

Virtually the entire Civil War was fought on Southern battlefields. Because of this, as the fighting reached ever deeper into Confederate territory, hundreds of Southern women of all social and economic classes had little choice but to ignore popular prejudice and become frontline nurses. Makeshift hospitals for the wounded were set up in churches, town halls, and train depots—even in private homes, if there was not enough public space. Janie Smith, the 18-year-old daughter of a wealthy North Carolina planter, was one Southerner who found herself drafted into service as a frontline nurse when the war literally came to her doorstep. Confederate troops fighting nearby transformed her family's estate into a field hospital in 1865. At first the scale of the carnage and suffering overwhelmed her:

"It makes me shudder when I think of the awful sights I witnessed that morning," Janie wrote to a friend. "Ambulance after ambulance drove up with our wounded. . . . Under every shed and tree, the tables were carried for amputating the limbs. . . . The blood lay in puddles in the grove; the groans of the dying and complaints of those undergoing amputation were horrible." By the end of the day, however, Smith overcame her initial squeamishness. This sheltered and genteel young Southern lady proudly informed her friend, "I could dress amputated limbs . . . and do most anything in the way of nursing wounded soldiers."

HARSH WORKING CONDITIONS AND TYRANNICAL DOCTORS

Whether in makeshift field hospitals bordering battlefields, or in general hospitals safely removed from the fighting, nurses on both sides of the conflict had to endure harsh working conditions. In her memoirs of her six-month stint at a Union hospital in Washington, D.C., author Louisa May Alcott effectively captured the heavy emotional burdens of wartime nursing. When she first saw the "legless, armless occupants" of the hospital ward to which she had been assigned, Alcott wrote, the only way she could keep her emotions under control was to scold herself "that I was there to work, not to wonder or weep."

Alcott and other Civil War nurses typically put in long, exhausting days—sometimes toiling for 16 hours at a stretch—dressing wounds, giving out medications, serving meals, and writing letters for patients. Many also found themselves taking on tasks such as scrubbing floors, emptying bedpans, or laundering sheets and hospital gowns. Often, there were so many casualties that there was no time for nurses to do their own laundry or even to change their clothes. Confederate nurse Kate Cumming recalled wearing the same dress for nine days straight when wounded soldiers began pouring into her Mississippi hospital following the bloody Battle of Shiloh in April 1862. When she was too exhausted to stay on her feet a minute longer, Cumming would simply stretch out fully clothed amongst a pile of boxes in the supply room and take a quick nap. Katherine Prescott Wormeley, who toiled on a busy Union Army transport ship, reported in a letter home:

> This matter of dirt and stains is becoming very serious. My dresses are in such a state that I loathe them, and myself in them. From chin to belt they are yellow with lemon-juice, sticky with sugar, greasy with beef-tea, and pasted with milk-porridge. Farther down, I dare not inquire into them. Somebody said the other day that he wished to kiss the hem of my garment. I thought of the condition of that article and shuddered.

Another challenge for many female nurses was their relationship with male hospital authorities. Kate Cumming, who eventually served as the matron of several Confederate hospitals, frequently found herself at odds with the institutions' male surgeons. Few of the men were prepared to recognize Cumming and her female staff as medical professionals. Cumming did, however, record one small "triumph for the ladies" in her diary during the summer of 1864. A nurse had developed a lotion to help reduce irritation and swelling, but the chief surgeon refused to recommend the lotion to his staff for the sole reason that "it had been made by a lady," Cumming reported. One of the hospital's physicians had been willing to give it a try, and when it proved effective, he requested more. "Such a simple acknowledgement of female competence warranted not just notice but celebration in Cumming's eyes," notes historian Nina Silber in *Daughters of the Union: Northern Women Fight the Civil War*.

Two Union nurses who dared to stand up to male hospital authorities were Hannah Ropes and Mary Ann Bickerdyke.

Ropes discovered that a male steward had been physically abusing several wounded soldiers at the hospital in Washington, D.C., where she worked. She immediately complained to the head surgeon. The surgeon, however, refused to take her word against that of his male employee. Ropes then boldly took the case to the secretary of war, who had the steward arrested. Bickerdyke, who served as a nurse and matron at more than 300 Union field hospitals during the war, clashed frequently with her superiors. Her most famous showdown took place at a hospital in Cairo, Illinois, when she publicly confronted a surgeon who had been stealing clothing meant for the patients. When the infuriated surgeon ordered her to leave the hospital at once, Bickerdyke boldly refused, causing her admiring patients to nickname her the "Cyclone in Calico." (Calico is a coarse, brightly printed cotton cloth that was often used in making women's clothing during the nineteenth century.)

THE RISKS AND REWARDS OF WARTIME NURSING

Clara Barton, who would become famous as the founder of the American Red Cross in 1881, was another woman not afraid to stand up to male authorities for what she believed was right. When the war broke out, Barton was working at the U.S. Patent Office in Washington, D.C., as one of the federal government's handful of female employees. She immediately began volunteering as a nurse. By the summer of 1861, she was collecting donated food, clothing, bandages, and other supplies, much of which she personally distributed to the soldiers on the front.

Convinced that she could be most useful to the Union troops on the battlefield, Barton stubbornly refused to follow military policies that barred women from the thick of the fighting. On several occasions, bullets ripped through Barton's clothing. During the Battle of Antietam in September 1862, at which more than 23,000 troops were killed or wounded, she was so close to the front lines that an injured soldier was shot dead in her arms as she gave him water. In recognition of Barton's unflinching courage, three months after Antietam, the army finally gave her formal permission to do what she had been doing for months anyway: tend to wounded troops directly on the battlefield.

Even for women assigned to general hospitals far removed from the front lines, Civil War nursing could be dangerous work. About twice as many Civil War soldiers died from illnesses as from battlefield wounds. As a result, military nurses were exposed to a wide range of potentially fatal diseases, such as pneumonia, influenza, measles, diphtheria, and typhoid fever. In January 1863, Louisa May Alcott nearly died from typhoid fever after catching it from one of her patients at the Union Hotel Hospital. Soon after Alcott's brush with death, Sally Gibbons, another Union hospital worker, paid tribute to a friend and fellow nurse who fell ill and died after tending to a sick soldier. "Who can say her life was not given to her country as truly as that of any one of the band of heroes who have fallen in battle?" Gibbons asked.

Despite the hardships, frustrations, and very real dangers of Civil War nursing, however, nurses took comfort in the belief that their work was vitally important to their nation's cause and to the suffering soldiers under their care. "We have scarcely anything to eat. I have had nothing but hard-tack [a dry biscuit made with only water and flour] and tea since I came . . . as the trains are all taken up carrying forage and ammunition to the front," Union nurse Cornelia Hancock wrote to her sister from a Virginia field hospital in 1864. Still, she concluded, "I never was better in my life: certain I am in my right place." Likewise, hospital matron Katherine Prescott Wormeley declared: "Let no one pity or praise us, no one can tell how sweet it is to be the drop of comfort to so much agony."

Soldiers, Scouts, Saboteurs, and Spies

It is well known that many Northern and Southern women served their side's cause as nurses or other hospital workers during the Civil War. It is considerably less well known that hundreds of women disguised themselves as men and fought as Union and Confederate soldiers between 1861 and 1865. The exact number of female Civil War soldiers is impossible to determine, but historians believe that there were at least 400 of them.

A variety of motives caused women to defy the official ban on female soldiers and enlist in the military. The most common motives appear to have been patriotism, a desire to remain close to a husband or sweetheart serving in the army, and a longing for adventure. The promise of a living wage also may have inspired some women to become soldiers. In the mid-nineteenth century United States, most jobs, and particularly well-paying ones, were closed to females. Women who worked outside their homes typically toiled as household servants for a few dollars per month. Even those women fortunate enough to secure better-paying factory jobs generally received lower wages than their male coworkers. Union Army soldiers were paid $13 per month. This was hardly a huge sum in an era when most American men earned between $10 and $20 monthly, but nonetheless, it was four times what the typical female household servant could make in a month.

SARAH EMMA EDMONDS, ALIAS PRIVATE FRANK THOMPSON

The most famous female soldier of the Civil War was Sarah Emma Edmonds, or Private Frank Thompson, as her comrades in the Union Army knew her. Born in 1841, Edmonds grew up on her parents' farm in the Canadian province of New Brunswick. When she was 17, Edmonds's father promised his daughter's hand in marriage to an elderly neighbor whom she detested. At a time when women were expected to obey their male relatives and stay close to home, Edmonds vowed to run away from the family farm and find a way to support herself.

When she saw an advertisement in a local newspaper for a traveling salesman position that offered a good wage as well as a chance to see something of the world, she was immediately interested. Since women were prohibited from applying for the sales job, Edmonds hatched a bold scheme to secure the position: She would disguise herself as a man and take a male alias. Edmonds got the job and worked as a book salesperson in eastern Canada for nearly two years under the name Franklin Thompson.

The always-restless Edmonds then decided to immigrate to the United States. She chose Flint, Michigan, as her home base, and she continued her successful sales career in her adopted country. Less than a year after settling in Michigan, Edmonds was shaken by reports of the Confederate capture of Fort Sumter. Strongly opposed to slavery, Edmonds asked herself, "What part am I to act in this great drama?" A month later, in May 1861, she made her decision: She would enlist in the 2nd Michigan

Hoping to have an active role in the war, Sarah Emma Edmonds disguised herself as a man and fought for the Union. Dressed in men's clothes, Edmonds passed a simple questions-only medical exam and fought in several battles, including First Bull Run. Though no one suspected her of being of woman, Edmonds was nicknamed "Our Woman" by her regiment for having feminine mannerisms.

Infantry Regiment as "Franklin Thompson." (Infantry soldiers fought on foot, while cavalry soldiers fought on horseback. Typically made up of 1,000 to 1,500 soldiers, the regiment was the basic military unit of the Civil War.)

Passing the entry medical examination proved easy for Edmonds, since Civil War military physicals usually consisted of little more than asking recruits a few questions about their current and past health. "I could only thank God that I was free and could go forward and work, and I was not obliged to stay at home and weep," she later wrote of her feelings upon being admitted into the Union Army. As a member of the 2nd Michigan Infantry, Edmonds fought in several major battles, including the First Battle of Bull Run in July 1861 (also known as the First Battle of Manassas) and Fredericksburg in December 1862. "Private Thompson," however, generally was given non-combat assignments, particularly as a regiment nurse, a job for which "he" appeared to have a great deal of natural skill.

In early 1863 Edmonds caught malaria, a serious disease passed to humans by mosquitoes. Edmonds realized that her deception was sure to be discovered if she sought medical treatment from the army. Because of this, Edmonds decided to desert. After nearly five years as Franklin Thompson, she quietly resumed her female identity and checked into a civilian hospital. Once she was cured, Edmonds traveled to Washington, D.C., to work as an army nurse.

Shortly before the war's end, Edmonds published a best-selling account of her Civil War experiences in which she claimed to have carried out several daring spy missions behind enemy lines. It is a matter of debate among historians as to whether Edmonds actually spied for the Union Army, since there is no evidence to back up her claim.

In 1884 Edmonds, by that time a married mother of three, successfully petitioned Congress for a veteran's pension. It was a highly unusual honor for a woman. In filing the petition, she had the backing of a number of her old comrades in the 2nd Michigan, who praised Private Thompson's outstanding "soldiering qualities" and "devotion to the sick." Edmonds was both touched and surprised by her comrades' unwavering support for her during her campaign to obtain a military pension. Notes Laura Leedy Gansler in *The Mysterious Private Thompson: The Double Life of Sarah Emma Edmonds, Civil War Soldier*:

At a time when the idea of women at war was so alien, it would have been understandable if they had reacted with anger and humiliation upon learning that a young woman had been among them in such intimate proximity. The fact that they embraced her cause so warmly is a testament to the affection and respect they felt for Frank Thompson, and their appreciation for the compassion and commitment "he" had shown to the sick and wounded during the war.

OTHER FAMOUS FEMALE SOLDIERS OF THE CIVIL WAR

Jennie Hodgers, who immigrated to the United States from Ireland as a child, holds the record for the longest documented term of service by a female soldier in the Civil War. Using the name Albert Cashier, 18-year-old Hodgers enlisted in the 95th Illinois Infantry in August 1862, and remained with her regiment until the war's end in the spring of 1865. At just 5 feet tall (1.5 m), Hodgers was definitely petite. Many Union Army volunteers were boys of 15 or 16, though, so Jennie's small stature failed to arouse her comrades' suspicions. During her three years with the 95th, Hodgers fought in dozens of battles and skirmishes, developing a reputation for exceptional courage under fire. After the war, Hodgers kept her male identity and eventually collected a military pension. Her secret was finally discovered in 1911, when a broken leg sent the 67-year-old to an Illinois veterans' hospital.

Although there are more documented cases of women enlisting with the Union than with the Confederacy, Southern women also assumed male identities and took up arms for their side. The most famous Confederate female soldier was Loreta Janeta Velazquez, a Cuban native who took the alias Harry T. Buford. Velazquez published a best-selling account of her war experiences in 1876, titled *The Woman in Battle*. In it, she claimed among other things to have fought in the front lines at the First Battle of Bull Run, risked her life repeatedly as a Confederate spy, and raised a 200-man cavalry volunteer company in Arkansas. (Led by a captain, Civil War–era companies usually were made up of no more than 100 soldiers.) For years, scholars viewed Velazquez's sensational narrative with deep skepticism. Yet recent research suggests that historians may have been too hasty in dismissing *The Woman in Battle*. Historians DeAnne Blanton and Lauren M. Cook point out that, although Velazquez clearly embellished some of her wartime adventures, newspaper articles, government documents, and other modern sources support key portions of her memoirs, including her presence at the First Battle of Bull Run.

Another well-known Confederate female soldier was Mary Ann Clark (also known as Amy Clarke). Clark's motivation for taking on a male alias and enlisting in the Confederate Army in 1861 is a matter of debate among historians. According to authors Blanton and Cook, Clark went to war to escape an unhappy marriage. Clark successfully kept up her masculine masquerade until she was wounded on a Kentucky battlefield and imprisoned by the Union for three months. Upon her release, Clark headed straight for Tennessee to join the army of Confederate General Braxton Bragg. When the details of Clark's story leaked out in late 1862, she became an unexpected celebrity and heroine in the South. Despite the region's deeply traditional ideas regarding women's proper role in society, the newspaper the *Mississippian* praised Clark for her courage and self-sacrifice. After taking part in battles in Tennessee and Kentucky, the newspaper reported, Clark was "wounded . . . [and] fell a prisoner into the hands of the Yankees. Her sex was discovered by the Federals, and she was regularly paroled as a prisoner of war, but they did not permit her to return until she had donned female apparel."

One female soldier who ended up fighting on both sides of the conflict was Malinda Blalock. Determined to stay near

Brave and daring, Loreta Janeta Velazquez donned men's clothing, rounded up 200 volunteers for a cavalry unit for the Confederate Army, and brought them to her husband's military camp in Florida. Known by the Confederacy as Lieutenant Harry T. Buford, Velazquez also worked as a spy and fought in some of the major battles of the Civil War.

her husband, Keith, Malinda enlisted in the 26th North Carolina Infantry with him, posing as Keith's brother "Samuel." Keith Blalock was a Union sympathizer and had felt pressured by his community to enlist. He and Malinda planned to desert the Confederate Army at the earliest opportunity. In April 1862, a surgeon treated Malinda for a shoulder wound and discovered she was a woman. It was clear she would be discharged anyway, so the couple switched sides, eventually joining the 10th Michigan Cavalry as "brothers" Keith and Samuel Blalock.

SCOUTS, MESSENGERS, GUIDES, AND SMUGGLERS

During the Civil War, Southern and Northern women broke out of traditional female roles not only by becoming soldiers, but also by serving—officially or unofficially—as scouts, messengers, guides, and smugglers. Many of these daring female patriots were hardly more than girls. Sixteen-year-old Melvina Stevens, for example, was a trusted scout for the famous Tennessee Unionist Dan Ellis. Ellis guided escapees from Southern military prisons, Confederate Army deserters, and fleeing slaves through the mountains of his native state to safety behind federal lines. In Virginia, teenager Nancy Hart, an expert horseback rider and marksman, provided invaluable assistance to the Confederacy as a scout, messenger, and guide. In 1862, after several Union soldiers took her prisoner, Hart managed to escape by shooting one of her captors with his own gun and then galloping off on his horse. The following year, another Southerner, 15-year-old Emma Sansom of Alabama, risked her life to pilot General Nathan Bedford Forrest and his cavalry regiment across a rain-swollen creek near her home after Union soldiers torched the stream's only bridge. In recognition of Sansom's heroic action, in 1864 the Alabama legislature awarded the teenager a gold medal.

Ongoing frustrations for the Union were the numerous women who smuggled prohibited items into the Confederacy, including weapons, and also medicine to treat the malaria and other illnesses that devastated the Confederate ranks. Only a few months after the war began, a Northern journalist warned that female smugglers sympathetic to the Confederacy already had snuck "hundreds if not thousands of pistols" past Union officials. Federal officers had no choice but to ignore the pleas of modest ladies who protested being searched, the journalist declared, advising: "Let her blush. Better that the blood should mount to her face than that the blood of our countrymen should be shed through her crime."

The majority of smuggling took place in the border states of Maryland, Missouri, and Tennessee, where the line between North and South was blurred. One of the most successful Confederate smugglers was Isabella "Belle" Edmondson, who lived near the port city of Memphis, Tennessee. Edmondson snuck equipment, uniforms, medical supplies, and dozens of other forbidden items past Union officials in and around Memphis for years. She usually concealed the contraband in her clothing. In her diary, Edmondson described a harrowing mission in March 1864 in which she carried so many items, including materials for Confederate uniforms, through Union lines that she had considerable trouble just walking:

> At one o'clock Mrs. Fackler, Mrs. Kirk & I began to fix my articles for smuggling. We made a [petticoat] of the Gray cloth for uniforms . . . tied the boots with a strong list, letting them fall directly in front. . . . All my letters, brass buttons, money & c in my bosom. . . . Started to walk, impossible that, hailed a hack [a hired coach]—rather suspicious of it, afraid of small-pox [a serious infectious disease], weight of contrabands ruled—jumped in with orders for a hurried drive to corner Main & Vance. . . . Arrived at Pickets [sentries' post], no trouble at all, although I suffered horribly in anticipation of trouble. Arrived home at dusk. . . .

Confederate and Union Spies
Antonia Ford and Frances Jamieson

Antonia Ford of Virginia began spying for the Confederacy soon after the war began and continued until her arrest two years later by Union agents in March 1863. Ford lived with her well-to-do family in Fairfax Court House, just outside Washington, D.C. Although they were actually strong supporters of Southern independence, the Fords pretended to be Unionists. Antonia's father opened his home to Union officers as a place to board and conduct government and military business. Antonia would then eavesdrop on the officers' conversations and forward whatever she heard about troop movements and other military matters to Confederate General J.E.B. Stuart and Colonel John S. Mosby. When Union Brigadier General Edwin Stoughton established headquarters near Antonia's Fairfax home, she carefully reported on his activities to Stuart and Mosby. In early March 1863 she played a critical role in assisting Mosby and his troops in their capture of Stoughton.

U.S. Secret Service head Lafayette Baker suspected the Fords of being involved in Stoughton's capture. To gain more information, Baker planted a female double agent in the Ford home with orders to gain the confidence of Antonia and her family. The agent, Frances Jamieson, or Frankie Abel, as she called herself, claimed to be a loyal Confederate who had been driven from her New Orleans home by Union troops. The Fords fell for Jamieson's story, and Antonia and "Frankie" soon became close friends. When Antonia proudly showed her new friend a commendation she had received from General Stuart for her assistance to the Confederate cause, Jamieson immediately informed Baker, who had Antonia arrested. She was placed in the Old Capitol Prison where, ironically, she fell in love with one of her Union interrogators, Major Joseph C. Willard. After signing an oath of loyalty to the Union, Ford was released from prison, and on March 10, 1864, she married the major. She and Willard had three children together before her untimely death in 1871 at the age of 33.

By the summer of 1864, Edmondson's frequent trips finally had aroused the suspicion of the Union authorities, who issued a warrant for her arrest. Fleeing southward, Edmondson settled on a remote plantation in Mississippi, where she remained until the war's end.

SABOTEURS

Some Southern women, particularly residents of border states, also strove to weaken the Union cause through sabotage. Sabotage is the destruction of property or interference of normal operations by civilians or undercover agents during wartime. "Saboteurs," notes Catherine Clinton in *Tara Revisited: Women, War, & the Plantation Legend*, were particularly useful to the Confederacy, "for they could commit acts that incapacitated and astonished the enemy." Missouri saboteur Katie Beattie, for example, torched dozens of Union boats and warehouses. In Tennessee, a "Mrs. Hunter" and her daughter confessed to slowing a Union advance by destroying several bridges near their home, boldly declaring to Union authorities that they would "do it again if given the chance."

Probably the best-known female saboteur of the Civil War was Sarah Jane Smith of Missouri. In autumn 1864, Smith was convicted by a Union military court of cutting down 4 miles (6.5 kilometers) of army telegraph wires. The telegraph used electricity to send written messages in code across wires strung between tall poles. Although Smith was just 18 years old at the time of her trial, she was sentenced to hang for her crime. Smith's sentence might seem excessively harsh, but both the Union and Confederate sides viewed the telegraph as vitally important to their military strategy, since it allowed field commanders to send reports and orders almost instantaneously over long distances.

By all accounts, young Sarah had a difficult life. Her mother died when Sarah was still a child. When her father joined the

Confederate Army in 1862, Sarah was left entirely on her own. She moved from her native Arkansas to Missouri to live with relatives. Once there, the 16-year-old quickly became involved with several older male cousins who talked her into helping them destroy Union telegraph lines near the city of Springfield. After her cousins were captured and imprisoned by Union officials during the summer of 1864, a local Confederate sympathizer offered Sarah five dollars to continue her sabotage work. Prior to that, Sarah had been living off the land with her cousins in the countryside near Springfield. In September, federal authorities caught the homeless teenager just outside Springfield cutting down army telegraph lines with an ax. They sentenced her to die the following November.

Less than two weeks before the sentence was to be carried out, however, Union officials called in two physicians to examine Smith, who apparently had been having seizures. The doctors concluded that Smith not only suffered from epilepsy, but also lacked "sufficient mental capacity to fully appreciate the crimes which she has committed" and therefore should not be held fully responsible for her actions. At the physicians' recommendation, Smith's sentence was changed to imprisonment until the end of the war. This allowed federal authorities "to avoid the stigma of hanging a woman," writes historian Thomas P. Lowry in *Confederate Heroines: 120 Southern Women Convicted by Union Military Justice.*

SPYING FOR THE CONFEDERACY

During the Civil War, a number of women sought to further their side's cause by spying. Sometimes this was done under the direct supervision of the Confederate or Union government or military, and in other instances women acted as freelance agents entirely on their own. Many of these female spies made vital contributions to their government's war effort, often risking their freedom or even their lives in the process. One of the most effective, daring, and resourceful of the Confederacy's female spies was Rose O'Neal Greenhow.

The widow of a distinguished Maryland physician, Greenhow was well known in upper-class social circles. At the start of the Civil War, she had been living for some time in Washington, D.C., where she had many friends and acquaintances in the federal government and the military. She was intelligent, attractive, and personable, and despite her known Southern sympathies, Greenhow managed to find out important military information from several of her Union acquaintances. In July 1861 she helped secure a Southern victory in the first major battle of the war, near Bull Run Stream, by passing vital information about Union strategy and troop strength to Confederate General Pierre G.T. Beauregard. In the wake of the Union defeat at Bull Run, the U.S. Secret Service, which had been watching Greenhow for weeks, placed the 44-year-old widow under house arrest. They later sent her to Old Capitol Prison, once a fashionable boardinghouse in the heart of Washington. Greenhow remained at Old Capitol Prison for five months, during which time she continued to communicate with Confederate agents, reportedly by hiding small messages inside the hair bun of a regular female visitor.

On May 31, 1862, exasperated Union officials finally deported Greenhow to the South. She was hailed as a heroine by President Jefferson Davis, who reportedly told her, "But for you there would have been no Battle of Bull Run." In 1863 Davis sent Greenhow to Europe to promote the Confederate cause as his unofficial representative. After one year, Greenhow sailed home on a British blockade-runner, a vessel designed to outmaneuver the Union patrol boats that guarded the waters off the Confederate coastline. The ship ran aground in stormy seas near Wilmington, North Carolina, and Greenhow, fearful of capture by Union patrollers, fled in a rowboat. The small boat capsized in the waves, and Greenhow drowned. In October 1864 she was buried in a Wilmington cemetery with full Confederate military honors.

Another celebrated Confederate female spy was Belle Boyd of Martinsburg, Virginia, who was just 18 when her spying career began. Vibrant and flirtatious, Boyd was remarkably skilled at charming military information out of the Union soldiers who occupied her hometown in July 1861. Although she usually sent her information through messengers, on one occasion she risked her life crossing military lines to hand deliver urgent information about Union troop movements to Confederate General Stonewall Jackson.

During the summer of 1862 the Union finally figured out what Belle was up to and sent her to the Old Capitol Prison, where she remained for one month before being freed in exchange for the Union's release of Confederate prisoners. The Union imprisoned her again in 1863 on suspicion of carrying messages for the enemy, but she was released after six months due to health concerns. In 1864, she set sail for Great Britain on a blockade-runner, carrying messages from Jefferson Davis, but her ship was captured off the U.S. coast by Union patrollers. The officer responsible for delivering Boyd to federal authorities was so smitten by her that he instead helped her escape to Canada. They were later married. After the war, Boyd launched a successful career as a lecturer, giving dramatic talks on her Civil War experiences in cities and towns across the United States—including in the North. She died in Wisconsin in 1900 during a lecture tour.

SPYING FOR THE UNION

The most colorful Union spy was actually a Southerner by birth: Pauline Cushman. Born in New Orleans and raised in the Midwest, Cushman was a stage actress in Kentucky during the early years of the war. In 1863 she was recruited by the Union to serve as a double agent for the North. It was widely known

An accomplished flirt, Southerner Belle Boyd used her considerable charm to trick Union soldiers into divulging sensitive military information. Repeatedly arrested for espionage, Boyd expressed her sympathies for the South by hanging the Confederate flag outside the train car taking her to prison and singing "Dixie" in her cell.

that Cushman had accepted a dare from an audience member to toast Jefferson Davis during one of her stage performances in Louisville. Because of this, it was easy for her to win the trust of the Confederates and to gain access to their military camps.

After visiting General Braxton Bragg's headquarters near Nashville, Tennessee, however, she was caught by the Confederates with incriminating documents in her possession. She was convicted of treason and sentenced to hang. Just days before the sentence was to be carried out, the Union Army of the Cumberland overran Bragg's headquarters and Cushman was saved from the gallows. In 1865, she published a sensational account of her wartime adventures entitled *The Life of Pauline Cushman*. When she died 28 years later in San Francisco, she was buried with military honors in recognition of her contributions to the Union cause.

An even more effective Southern-born spy for the Union side was Elizabeth Van Lew. Although the daughter of a wealthy Richmond slave owner, by the beginning of the Civil War, Van Lew had come to despise slavery and was strongly pro-Union. Because she seemed harmless, Confederate officials refused to believe that Van Lew could be passing along valuable military information to the Union Army, even though there was plenty of evidence to the contrary. Much of this intelligence came from a resourceful and courageous former family slave named Mary Elizabeth Bowser, whom Van Lew managed to plant as a servant in the Confederate White House.

After Van Lew's death in 1900, Northern admirers placed a stone marker at her Richmond grave with the following inscription: "She risked everything that is dear to man—friends, fortune, comfort, health, life itself—all for the one absorbing desire of her heart, that slavery might be abolished and the Union preserved."

Women in Camp

Thousands of women attached themselves to the Union and Confederate Armies during the war. These women included the wives, sweethearts, and mothers of soldiers; laundresses; and "sutlers," the civilians who sold sweets, crackers, pickles, tobacco, and other small luxuries to soldiers in camp. It may seem surprising that so many female civilians participated in camp life. Yet, as Elizabeth D. Leonard notes in *All the Daring of a Soldier: Women of the Civil War Armies*, "By the time of the Civil War, the presence of women in and around the army was hardly a path breaking development." The practice of women living, working, and traveling with armies had been common in Europe for centuries. In the United States during the Revolutionary War (1775–1783), the Continental Army had teemed with the female relatives of soldiers.

LAUNDRESSES, SUTLERS, AND "CAMP FOLLOWERS"

Women were drawn to Civil War military encampments for a variety of reasons. These included a desire to be near loved ones, patriotism, a yearning for adventure, and the promise of earning a steady income as a regimental laundress or a sutler.

Laundresses were present in virtually every Union and Confederate Army camp. Companies appointed their own military laundresses, usually 4 women for a unit of 100 men. In camps where an especially tidy appearance was emphasized, regular laundry service was considered a necessity. Doing laundry was a considerably more time-consuming and labor-intensive task in the days before electric- or gas-powered washing machines, dryers, and irons existed. Because of this, few soldiers had either the time or the desire to wash and press their own uniforms. Most army washerwomen came from lower-class backgrounds. Although their work was backbreaking and tedious, the pay and benefits that came with a laundress position more than made up for the job's drawbacks. Military laundresses were paid in cash for their labors by their soldier clients and also received regular soldiers' rations and lodgings from the army. "If a woman charged a soldier as little as fifty cents per month for his laundry, assuming that a company of 100 men had four washerwomen, her monthly earning could almost equal those of a private," writes Virginia Mescher in " 'Under the Canopy of Heaven': Military Laundresses in the Civil War." Laundresses, Mescher notes, also could earn extra cash by mending soldiers' clothing.

Although most Civil War sutlers were male, women also sometimes followed the troops for the purpose of selling food, liquor, cloth, and other items to the men. The majority of these female peddlers worked with their husbands, but a few, such as Mary Tepe (sometimes spelled Tebe), were independent agents. In April 1861, Tepe, a French immigrant to the United States, followed her husband, a Philadelphia tailor named Bernardo, into the 27th Pennsylvania Infantry. To support herself, she set up shop as a sutler. By late 1862, Mary had transferred to another Pennsylvania regiment, the 114th, apparently after a falling-out with her husband over money. She stayed with the 114th for the rest of the war, adding to her income as a sutler by cooking and sewing for the men in her unit. When the 114th went to battle, Tepe loyally volunteered to serve as a water carrier for her regiment, risking her life to bring canteens of water to the thirsty, weary troops. After being wounded in the leg at the Battle of Fredericksburg in December 1862, she was awarded the Kearney Cross for bravery under fire.

Another group of women who sought to support themselves by traveling with the Union and Confederate Armies were prostitutes, or "camp followers," as they were commonly known at the time. According to military regulations, camp followers were supposed to have periodic medical examinations to ensure that they were not infected with syphilis, a serious sexually transmitted disease that had no cure until the discovery of penicillin in 1928. Many prostitutes failed to follow this rule, however, and syphilis was common among Northern and Southern troops alike. Indeed, the disease was probably being spread from one Civil War army to another since it was not unusual for camp followers to drift back and forth between Union and Confederate camps in war-torn areas. "The armies sometimes moved out of an area so rapidly that the prostitutes were left behind," writes historian Mary Elizabeth Massey, "but those traveling with the Federals usually caught up and those with the retreating Confederates often awaited the foe."

JOINING LOVED ONES IN CAMP

Wives and other female relatives of enlisted men generally were discouraged from attaching themselves to army camps on both the Confederate and Union sides for prolonged periods.

Although less exciting and glamorous than espionage or battlefield action, domestic chores for soldiers became the paid work of choice for many women. Providing laundry service to a unit of men became a profitable business for many women who had to support their families during the war. Laundresses, like the one above, and sutlers were part of the support system for both the North and the South during the Civil War.

Exceptions were made for official laundresses or cooks. Officers' wives, however, could and did spend more time in camp. Some officers forbade their wives from joining them because of the potential dangers, primitive conditions, and often crude talk of army life.

Others, such as General Benjamin Butler of the Union Army, had their wives with them as much as possible during the war. Butler once said he was grateful for the presence of his wife, Sarah, in camp, not only because she made a home for him wherever the army traveled, but also because she was his "trusted" adviser, "faithful, true, and clearheaded, conscientious and conservative." Other wives who spent much of the Civil War traveling and living with their officer husbands included General Ulysses S. Grant's wife, Julia Dent Grant, and Confederate General Bradley Johnson's wife, Jane Claudia Johnson.

Even though the wives and other female relatives of enlisted men typically were unwelcome at camp except for brief visits, female relations of soldiers who were recovering from an illness or wound often were permitted to stay in camp with their loved ones for extended periods. When units moved toward the front, however, these women were almost always left behind. This often resulted in their being stranded many miles from home. A Union soldier described the sad plight of an impoverished Irish immigrant and her baby who were abandoned in this way in northern Virginia:

> I overtook a young Irish woman that had come away here from Pennsylvania at Pittsburgh to see her husband willing to follow him as he fought for his country but when his regiment came to embark at Alexandria [Virginia] to go farther South they would not let her go any farther[,] drove her back[:] she was but poorly thinly clad she & an infant some nine or ten months old in her arms, both mother & child shivering & crying with the cold. . . . She had nothing but the charities of the soldiers and warm womans love to cheer and sustain her passage back to her desolate home, such cases are not rare. . . .

VIVANDIÈRES

In middle- and upper-class "respectable" society during the Civil War era, it was generally considered improper for a single woman to attach herself to the army, even as a nurse, cook, or laundress. An exception to this rule was the vivandière, who might be a young unmarried woman or the wife of a soldier. *Vivandière* was originally a French term for a woman who accompanied an army regiment to sell goods. She wore a feminized version of the regiment's uniform with a knee-length skirt over the pants and extra braiding or decorative buttons on the jacket.

In the Civil War, vivandières, or "daughters of the regiment," as they were also known, were not expected to act as sutlers. Instead, they were a kind of regiment mascot. The American vivandières typically were outfitted in colorful, military-style uniforms featuring full skirts over baggy trousers, short jackets, and jaunty hats. At first they were entrusted with ceremonial duties only, such as carrying flags in parades and reviews. More often than not, daughters of the regiment were related to an officer or enlisted man, who was expected to act as the vivandière's chaperone or guardian. Attitudes toward vivandières differed widely from regiment to regiment. Some officers viewed them as an interference and as an unnecessary distraction, while others welcomed the women as morale boosters.

As the fighting intensified in early 1862, the number and roles of the vivandières changed dramatically. The majority of the daughters of the regiment were either sent home by their regimental officers or, horrified by the grim realities of war, left voluntarily. Most of those few who did stay on became nurses, caring for their unit's sick at camp and tending to the wounded on the battleground. The women's courage and self-sacrifice were greatly appreciated by the soldiers they served. For example, Eliza Wilson, a vivandière for the 5th Wisconsin, considered her chief duties to be comforting and soothing "the thirst of the wounded and dying on the battlefield." She was "worshipped by the rough soldiers . . . and held in high esteem by all the officers," according to a contemporary account.

ANNIE ETHERIDGE

Northern daughters of the regiment, such as Eliza Wilson, were not only heroines to the members of their units. During and immediately after the war, they received a great deal of favorable attention from the press for their bravery, endurance, and devotion to their regiments and to the Union cause. One of the most celebrated vivandières of the Civil War era was Annie Etheridge. Born in Detroit, Michigan, in 1844, Annie married James Etheridge in 1860 when she was just 16 years old. A year later in June 1861, Annie followed James to war as a daughter of the regiment when he enlisted in the 2nd Michigan Volunteer Infantry. James deserted during the early months of the war, but Annie stayed. She soon transferred to the 3rd Michigan (later absorbed into the 5th Michigan) to serve as that regiment's vivandière.

As Richard Hall notes in *Patriots in Disguise: Women Warriors of the Civil War*, when she signed up, Annie "had no intention of being a mere parade ground ornament." Over the course of the nearly four years that she served as a vivandière, Etheridge directly participated in many of the war's bloodiest battles, including the First Battle of Bull Run in 1862, Chancellorsville and Gettysburg in 1863, and Spotsylvania Court House in 1864. Giving medical aid and comfort to her comrades on the battlefield, she believed, was her most critical duty as a daughter of the regiment. "Armed with a pair of pistols stuck in her belt," writes Richard Hall, Annie made her usual battle post "just behind the lines attended by the surgeon's orderly who carried a medicine chest."

Etheridge's devotion to the troops ran so deep that she was always prepared to expose herself to direct enemy fire to save a soldier's life. "Many times when Annie saw a man fall wounded, she would dash forward into the hottest part of the battle, lift the wounded soldier onto her horse, and carry him safely to the rear where he could receive prompt care," writes Hall. On a number of occasions, shell fragments or bullets tore Annie's clothing, but this failed to stop her from carrying out her missions of mercy. "Passing under fire, regardless of shot and shell, engaged in the work of staunching blood and binding up wounds, . . . she never flinched," a journalist wrote admiringly of Etheridge in 1863.

During the thick of battle, Etheridge did not hesitate to take on a leadership role within her regiment, if she thought it was necessary. On several different occasions she rallied the troops, including at the bloody Spotsylvania Court House campaign in Virginia in May 1864. Annie scolded a group of fleeing soldiers there to do their duty, and then personally led them back into the fray under heavy Confederate fire. She was always ready to share every hardship as well as every danger with the men in her regiment. One young Union recruit who encountered Etheridge near Chancellorsville, Virginia, in 1863 noted in his diary:

> Commenced to rise about daylight, and the first thing that greeted our optics was a female rising up from the ground. It was none other than that heroine of the War, Annie Etheridge, and a braver soul cannot be found. She is always on hand and ready to bear the same privations [hardships] as the men. When danger threatens she never cringes. At the battle of Fredericksburg she was binding the wounds of a man when a shell exploded nearby, tearing him terribly, and removing a large portion of the skirt of her dress. This morning she was surrounded by soldiers on every side, laying outside with no covering but her blanket, but such lodgings must have been selected voluntarily, for there isn't a man at any of the headquarters who wouldn't gladly surrender his bed and tent to her.

After the war, the U.S. Treasury Department offered Etheridge a full-time position based largely on the glowing letters of recommendation that her former comrades wrote for her, in which they lavishly praised her character and work ethic. When treasury officials dismissed her in 1878 in order to give her position to a male worker, angry Union veterans flooded the department with letters, demanding that Etheridge's job be returned to her. Etheridge did not get her job back, but in 1887 Congress awarded her a military pension of $25 per month.

KADY BROWNELL

Another daughter of the regiment who was widely praised by both the Union troops and the Northern press was Kady Brownell of Rhode Island. She was the daughter of a Scottish soldier, and after her mother's death Kady was sent to the United States from Great Britain to live with family friends. In March 1861, when she was 18 years old, Kady married Robert Brownell, a millwright. (A millwright was a workman who made or repaired machinery used in a mill, where raw materials were turned into finished or industrial products.)

Soon after the Confederate attack on Fort Sumter, Robert Brownell joined the 1st Rhode Island Volunteer Infantry, transferring to the 5th Rhode Island a few months later. Determined to stay close to her husband, Kady Brownell convinced both regiments to designate her as their vivandière. Rumored to be an excellent marksman, Brownell carried both a rifle and a saber and was frequently permitted to drill and train with the soldiers. Like Annie Etheridge, she shared every hardship with the men in her unit, marching alongside them and sleeping on the hard ground with a knapsack for a pillow. Her dedication and fortitude convinced the 5th Rhode Islanders to designate the teenager as their color bearer, meaning that she was responsible for carrying the regiment's flag into combat. Being named regimental color bearer was an unusual honor for a vivandière. Carrying the regimental banner was also a highly dangerous duty since the large banner could usually be counted on to draw plenty of enemy fire.

A Dying Soldier's Tribute to Annie Etheridge

At the Battle of Chancellorsville on May 2 to 3, 1863, Annie Etheridge was in the field hospital nursing the wounded when she stumbled upon a seriously wounded soldier who had some-how been overlooked by the surgeons. She gave the man water, bound up his wounds, and tried her best to comfort him. Nearly a year later she received a letter from the injured soldier, who turned out to be George Hill of Cleveland, Ohio. The letter was apparently written as Hill lay dying in a hospital in Washington, D.C. It read:

Washington, D.C., January 14th, 1864

Annie—Dearest Friend:

I am not long for this world, and I wish to thank you for your kindness 'ere I go.

You were the only one who was ever kind to me, since I entered the Army. At Chancellorsville, I was shot through the body, the ball entering my side, and coming out through the shoulder. I was also hit in the arm, and was carried to the hospital in the woods, where I lay for hours, and not a surgeon would touch me; when you came along and gave me water, and bound up my wounds. I do not know what regiment you belong to, and I don't know if this will ever reach you. There is only one man in your division that I know. I will try and send this to him; his name is Strachan, orderly sergeant in Sixty-third Pennsylvania volunteers.

But should you get this, please accept my heartfelt gratitude; and may God bless you, and protect you from all dangers; may you be eminently successful in your present pursuit. . . . I know nothing of your history, but I hope you always have, and always may be happy; and since I will be unable to see you in this world, I hope I may meet you in that better world, where there is no war. May God bless you, both now and forever, is the wish of your grateful friend.

Brownell's claim to fame came on a foggy day in the spring of 1862, when she was serving with the 5th Rhode Islanders at the Battle of New Bern in North Carolina. Suddenly Brownell saw a group of sharpshooters from another Union regiment taking direct aim at her comrades, their view obscured by the fog and the thick battle smoke. Brownell responded instantly, running right in front of the shooters and frantically signaling the soldiers with her flag to hold their fire. Brownell's comrades were saved by her courageous act, and she became an instant heroine among the troops and in the Northern press, which gave wide coverage to her inspiring and dramatic story.

As it turned out, New Bern would be the last Civil War battle in which Kady Brownell participated, since Robert Brownell was seriously injured during the fighting and was forced to take a medical discharge from the army. According to some accounts, when the Brownells were officially discharged, Major General Ambrose Burnside, commander of the Union forces at New Bern, personally presented a sergeant's sword to the courageous 19-year-old with "Kady Brownell" inscribed on the blade sheath.

LUCY ANN COX

The most famous Confederate vivandière of the Civil War was Lucy Ann Cox of the 30th Virginia Infantry Regiment, who followed her husband, James, to war in 1861. At first the 30th Virginia's officers, who strongly disapproved of wives accompanying the troops, ordered her to stay clear of the camp. But Lucy Cox was not the kind of person to give up easily. Determined to stay as close to her husband as possible, Cox responded to the officers' order by defiantly setting up a small tent for herself on the camp's outskirts. Soon Cox's usefulness as a volunteer seamstress, her popularity among the enlisted men, and her steady determination convinced the officers to bend their rules regarding women in camp.

Vivandières served as female mascots to the units of soldiers in the military. Known as "daughters of the regiment," these women were at first given only ceremonial duties, such as serving as flag carriers in parades. Later, as the fighting intensified, most of the vivandieres who remained with their regiments became nurses. Some vivandieres, like Annie Etheridge of Michigan, became famous during the war for their remarkable courage under fire and devotion to their regiments.

Cox was designated the 30th Virginia's "daughter." For four years, until the war's end, Cox lived and traveled with the 30th Virginia Infantry, accompanying her husband and his comrades into battle time and time again as a nurse and water carrier. "Throughout her service," writes historian Elizabeth Leonard, Cox "repeatedly demonstrated her willingness to suffer as the men suffered, to march as they marched (usually refusing offers to ride in the regiment's ambulances or wagon trains), and to respond with . . . good cheer to every request for assistance from every Confederate soldier she encountered, though she reserved her most devoted attention for her own company."

In appreciation for her tireless service to the 30th Virginia, after the war Cox was elected as an honorary member of the local veteran's group in Fredericksburg, Virginia, where she and her husband made their home. When she died in 1891, Cox was buried in the Fredericksburg Confederate Cemetery with full military honors. The inscription on her gravestone testifies to the high regard in which the grateful Southern soldiers held her: "Lucy Ann Cox . . . A sharer of the toils, danger and privations of the 30th Regiment Virginia Infantry, C.S.A. from 1861–1865 and died beloved and respected by the veterans of that command."

Northern Women During the Civil War

Over the past century and a half, popular and scholarly accounts of the Civil War alike have focused a great deal of attention on the thousands of female nurses, soldiers, vivandières, scouts, and spies who served their governments and armed forces during the conflict. The vast majority of American women, however, spent the war years at home. For these women, as for their sisters in military hospitals and camps, the war brought daunting new challenges and hardships.

This was true even for those who lived in the North, where few Civil War battles were fought. Between 1861 and 1865, more than 2 million Northern men enlisted in the Union Army. The absence of so many husbands, sons, fathers, brothers, and sweethearts created heavy emotional and economic burdens for the women left behind. Yet the men's participation in the war also provided unprecedented opportunities for many Union women to develop a new sense of independence and confidence in their own abilities through their involvement in soldier relief efforts or in managing the family farm or business.

The "Government Girls"

The expansion of the federal government and the absence of hundreds of male workers during the Civil War provided new employment opportunities for women to work as clerks, currency counters, and copyists for the national government. These positions were ones that men had dominated before 1861. "Government girls," as the women were nicknamed, were typically paid one-half of what their male counterparts received. Even that amount was considerably more than they could expect to earn as schoolteachers or in other traditionally female professions.

The largest employer of "government girls" between 1861 and 1865 was the Treasury Department. Francis Spinner, the head of the Treasury Department during and immediately after the Civil War, strongly supported the hiring of female office workers. Female clerks, he argued, were every bit as efficient as their male counterparts and much less expensive, since the federal government paid them only 50 percent of what it paid male employees. By the end of the war, the Treasury Department had hired 447 women. Several hundred more women worked in other federal offices, including the Patent Office, the Postal Service, and the Department of the Interior and Department of War.

Although many women would lose their jobs to returning soldiers after the war, the door had been opened to female government workers. By the end of the nineteenth century, notes historian Mary Elizabeth Massey, "women's position in government offices had been secured."

"TAKE YOUR GUN AND GO, JOHN"

From the very beginning of the war, the Northern press told women that the single most critical service they could give to their nation was to encourage their male relations to enlist in the military. For example, an 1861 editorial in *Arthur's Home*

Magazine, a popular periodical aimed at female readers, challenged Northern mothers to model themselves after the women of the Revolutionary War era, whose devotion to their young nation was legendary. Those self-sacrificing ladies, the editorial claimed, sent their sons off to fight in the Revolutionary War without complaint. The women understood that nothing—even the bond between a mother and her child—outweighed loyalty to one's homeland. "Our own mothers," the magazine's editors asserted, "are equal to their high duty, and strong enough for any sacrifice the country, in this hour of its trial, may demand."

The Union's early war propaganda also urged Northern wives to fulfill their patriotic responsibilities by supporting their husbands' decisions to enlist, regardless of the potential emotional or financial costs to themselves and their families. A cartoon in the popular journal *Harper's Weekly* suggested that Union ladies who selfishly tried to hold their husbands back from military service risked turning them into unmanly sissies. "He shouldn't go to the horrid war, away from his 'wifey, tifey,'" coos a large woman to her much smaller husband in the *Harper's* cartoon. "He shall have a petticoat and a broom, and stay at home."

In attempting to persuade women to send their spouses off to fight—and possibly die—for their country, the words to a popular Union song composed in 1861 took a very different approach from the *Harper's* cartoon. Instead of trying to shame wives into giving up their spouses, the lyrics to "The Volunteer's Wife to Her Husband" presented women with an inspirational role model for the virtuous Northern wife. The fictional "volunteer's wife" urges her husband to serve "as our beloved country's shield," and she nobly seeks to calm his concerns about abandoning his family. She reassures him that she and the children will be all right, no matter what the future might bring:

> *Don't stop a moment to think, John,*
> *Your country calls—then go;*

Don't think of me or the children, John,
I'll care for them, you know. . . .
And if it be God's will, John,
You ne'er come back again,
I'll do my best for the children, John,
In sorrow, want, and pain.
In winter nights I'll teach them all
That I have learned at school,
To love the country, keep the laws,
Obey the Savior's rule.
Then take your gun and go, John
Take your gun and go. . . .

Wartime propaganda also urged young unmarried women in the North to cheer on sweethearts and potential suitors who were contemplating enlistment. Men who tried to get out of their duty to the Union were to be strictly shunned. In her Civil War memoirs, Septima Collis, the wife of a Union officer, recalled that in her hometown of Philadelphia, the young women took this message to heart, "declaring they would never engage themselves to a man who refused to fight for his country." Farther north in Auburn, New York, 21-year-old Ellen Wright echoed the sentiments of the Philadelphia belles. After the First Battle of Bull Run in July 1861, she vowed that she would not even so much as "look at" any suitor who refused to enlist.

Not every young woman in the North shared this disdain for men who hesitated to enlist. For example, shortly after the Confederate attack on Fort Sumter, Lizzie Little of Illinois penned an impassioned letter to her fiancée, George Avery, pleading with him to delay his enlistment plans. As her letter makes clear, Lizzie did not share the nearly universal belief among Northerners during the early months of the conflict that the Confederacy would quickly fall in the face of Union military and economic might: "But George if I am allowed to say anything," she wrote, "do not go yet, wait. Let some battles be fought, see the power you have to contend with, for I believe it is a fierce one. The South will not be conquered in a day as some here vauntingly boast. . . ."

SOLDIERS' AID SOCIETIES

During the first weeks and months of the war, women on the Northern home front quickly realized that encouraging men to enlist was not all they could do to aid the war effort. Determined to help supply the rapidly growing Union Army, women across the North organized thousands of local soldiers' aid societies or ladies' aid societies, as they were also known, during the spring and summer of 1861. Meeting in public halls, churches, or private homes, the women knit socks, scarves, and gloves, sewed uniforms and regimental flags, rolled cloth bandages, and picked or scraped lint for packing wounds.

Lint, a soft material created by picking at worn cotton or linen fabric or scraping the material with a knife, was in high demand throughout the Civil War for packing battle wounds. Wads of moist lint were placed directly on the wound to keep it open and to promote proper drainage, and then it was covered with a cloth bandage kept in place by adhesive plaster. In her diary, 21-year-old Rebecca Loraine Richmond of Grand Rapids, Michigan, described helping her local "Ladies Aid Society" produce lint and a variety of other supplies for the 3rd Michigan Infantry Regiment, which was staying in her hometown during the spring of 1861. In addition to "a large quantity of lint and bandages," the items included 800 "housewives" (small bags filled with needles, pincushions, thread, and buttons for emergency mending jobs), 20 hospital gowns for the sick and wounded, and a "beautiful" hand-sewn "strand of color" or regimental flag, produced "according to Army Regulations, of blue silk, with yellow fringe, cord and tassels, and the State arms embroidered on both sides in yellow silk," as Rebecca noted proudly.

Northern aid societies usually did more than just produce supplies for soldiers. They also served as clearinghouses for donated goods for the troops. Aid society volunteers collected, sorted, packed, and shipped out the donated items along with any supplies they made themselves. In deciding where to send the supplies, many looked for guidance from the only national soldiers' aid society to be officially approved by the federal government, the U.S. Sanitary Commission. Working closely with the Union Army, the USSC informed the various aid societies of just which types of items—clothing, bedding, food, or medical supplies—were most needed by the various regiments and hospitals, and it made sure that they reached their intended destinations as rapidly as possible.

Many local aid societies in the North, either on their own or along with the USSC, also sponsored fund-raising events. These events ranged from large fairs to musical concerts and lectures. Their chief goal was to obtain money for purchasing supplies for the soldiers. Some of the women's fund-raising efforts were truly impressive in scope. In 1863, for instance, a group of female volunteers from Illinois helped organize and run a giant fair in Chicago with the support of the Northwestern Sanitary Commission. Hardworking and resourceful, "they traveled hundreds of miles to arouse the interest of Midwestern women, and dispatched 'seventeen bushels' of letters and circulars advertising the affair and urging donations," reports historian Mary Elizabeth Massey. In response, aid groups and individuals in Illinois and nearby states generously donated thousands of items, ranging from costly jewelry and works of art to handmade mittens and homegrown vegetables. The flood of contributions allowed the fair to go on for two weeks, eventually earning the Sanitary Commission a grand total of $100,000.

The president of the USSC, Rev. Henry W. Bellows, once declared that Union women were critical to the federal war effort. Above all, he maintained, it was vitally important that the

Women who were not directly assisting the soldiers in hospitals or on the battlefields were often active members of local aid organizations. Through their participation in local chapters of the U.S. Sanitary Commission (above), these women organized fund-raising fairs and collected and shipped supplies to hospitals and regiments at the front. Although most of the officials in the commission were men, women were the driving force in the local chapters.

North's tens of thousands of local soldiers' aid societies "rendered their immense service to the national struggle." Indeed, soldiers' aid volunteers had reason to be proud of their role in supplying the massive Union Army with clothing, hospital necessities, foodstuffs, and other crucial items during the war. "In private reflections and in public reports," notes Nina Silber in *Daughters of the Union: Northern Women Fight the Civil War,* "women spoke of the work as a welcome and significant expression of their patriotism, a vehicle that demonstrated their support for and interest in the war. Lacking the military and political outlets that men had, many women derived satisfaction from being able to make a contribution to the soldiers in the field."

ECONOMIC CHALLENGES

During the Civil War the absence of the main, and often the only, breadwinner from hundreds of thousands of Union households created unprecedented economic challenges for women on the Northern home front. In order to support themselves and their households, many Northern women ventured beyond their customary sphere of home and hearth to take up new economic roles on the farm, in the factory, or with the federal government.

American women of modest means always had toiled side by side with their male comrades in the fields, particularly during the hectic harvest seasons. During the Civil War, however, more Northern women than ever before, including many from more prosperous farming families, found themselves hoeing, planting, and harvesting food crops and tending livestock. For many rural Northern women, ensuring the economic well-being of their families while husbands, fathers, and brothers were gone at war meant a willingness to assume a variety of farming chores in addition to their usual housekeeping and childcare responsibilities.

From 1862 until 1863, for example, 24-year-old Mary Austin Wallace of Girard, Michigan, maintained a grueling schedule caring for her two young children and running the 160-acre (65-hectare) family farm while her husband, Bruce, fought with the Union Army. Wallace's wartime diary chronicles exhausting days filled with tasks once done by her husband, such as cutting corn, chopping firewood, putting up fences to protect crops from the neighbors' livestock, selling cattle, and keeping detailed accounts of expenses and earnings. This was on top of her normal domestic duties of soap-making, baking, weaving, sewing, and tending to her children.

Northern women who lived in cities and towns often turned to factory work to support themselves and their families. Hundreds of thousands of male factory workers volunteered for military service or were drafted after the draft began in the North in 1863. The absence of these men, combined with the demands of wartime production, brought never-before-seen numbers of female laborers into factories and mills. Many of the factory positions held by Northern women during the war were in government arsenals, where bullets, cartridges, fuses, percussion caps, and other munitions were manufactured.

Female munitions workers typically were paid less than their male counterparts. Still, their wages were considerably higher than those received by most domestic servants, seamstresses, schoolteachers, and women employed in other traditionally female occupations. There was one major drawback to munitions work, however: It could be extremely dangerous. Dozens of explosions and fires occurred in arsenals during the war, leaving scores of female workers seriously injured or dead.

One of the worst explosions was in September 1862 in the Allegheny Arsenal in Pittsburgh, Pennsylvania. Nearly 80 workers, most of them female, were killed. The victims' families, many of whom had depended heavily on the women's incomes, suffered more than just emotional trauma as a result of the accident. As Scott Nelson and Carol Sheriff point out in *A People at War: Civilians and Soldiers in America's Civil War*: "Although in 1862 Congress had approved pensions for the surviving dependents of soldiers who died as a direct result of military service, government officials rebuffed all requests to compensate families of the women killed at the Allegheny Arsenal." By "denying pensions to the families of deceased victims, as well as those maimed or disabled in the arsenal blast, government officials revealed their underlying assumption: that women were economic dependents, not breadwinners," contend Nelson and Sheriff.

Whether the federal government chose to acknowledge it or not, significant numbers of Northern women did become

Women and the New York City Draft Riot

The U.S. Congress passed the first national draft law, the Federal Enrollment Act, in the spring of 1863. After the act was passed, anti-draft protests erupted in a number of Northern towns and cities. Working class and poor Northerners were particularly angry over the new law because it permitted men to buy their way out of the draft by hiring substitutes. This option was well beyond the financial reach of poor and working-class men. Women played major roles in the anti-draft demonstrations, including involvement in what was by far the largest and bloodiest of the protests: the New York City draft riots of July 1863.

From July 13 to July 16, the rioters, most of whom were impoverished Irish immigrants, looted and torched the homes and businesses of wealthy New Yorkers. They also brutalized the city's black population, whom they viewed as their chief competitors for jobs. Eyewitness accounts indicate that women were among the most violent participants in the four-day-long riots. One group of female immigrants viciously beat a police officer, nearly killing him, according to some accounts. Others took part in the torching of a black orphanage and the lynching of African-American men. Federal troops, freshly arrived from the famous Battle of Gettysburg in Pennsylvania, finally stopped the riot on July 16. By that time, 105 lives had been lost in the struggle. In the aftermath of the riots, dozens of female and male New Yorkers were convicted of robbery, arson, and other crimes and were sent to prison.

their families' chief breadwinners when husbands and other male relatives went to war. Soaring wartime inflation rates left female breadwinners at the bottom of Northern society feeling particularly burdened by their new economic responsibilities. Between 1860 and 1864, food, clothing, and fuel prices rose in the North by about 80 percent. During the same period, wages typically rose by only 40 percent. This meant that as inflation consumed more and more of their earnings, poor women were hard-pressed to provide even the bare necessities of life for their families. No group struggled more than lower-class urban women. Unlike their rural counterparts, poor urban women lacked opportunities to grow any of their own food or chop their own firewood for fuel. Although assistance from federal or state governments was often available, obtaining the funds could be a long and complicated process. "Many who were eligible for aid meted [given] out to soldiers' dependents or to a part of the men's pay or to a widow's pension waited an interminable period before receiving compensation," notes Mary Elizabeth Massey, "and some did not know what they were entitled to or how to go about applying for it."

EMOTIONAL CHALLENGES: "THE HARDER PART OF WAR"

Women on the Union home front coped with emotional as well as economic challenges during the Civil War. They fought intense loneliness and anxiety over the fate of their loved ones in the military. Yet in the name of keeping up soldier morale, Northern women were strongly discouraged from sharing these emotional burdens with their men on the front. For example, in 1864, after the war already had been dragging on for three years, Mary Eleanor McCoy delivered a speech to her local women's patriotic league in Illinois, asking women to write "encouraging letters" to their loved ones in uniform. "Never write in a desponding tone," she said. "Wife, tell your husband how nicely you are getting along, if you have troubles keep them to yourself." An editorial in the popular periodical *Atlantic Monthly* gave its female readers more detailed advice about what they should and should not write to their men in the Union Army. Do not dwell on your fears, insecurities, or loneliness, the editorial directed. Instead, the article urged: "Be unwearying in details of the little interests of home. Fill your letters with kittens and canaries, with Baby's shoes, and Johnny's sled. . . . Keep him posted on all the village-gossip, the lectures, the courtings, the sleigh-rides, and the singing school. Bring out the good points of the world in sharp relief."

Despite these instructions to women, the actual letters of Union wives, mothers, and sweethearts to absent loved ones indicate that not all Northern women tried to maintain an encouraging or lighthearted tone in their letters. "I shall feel anxious till I hear from you after the battle," confessed Diana Phillips of Maine in a letter to her husband, Marshall, in 1862. "Good night from your anxious wife anxious for your safe arrival home." In Harriet Jane Thompson's sad note to her husband, a major in an Iowa volunteer regiment, she revealed that ever since his enlistment, she had spent many a restless night fretting about his health. "Oh, how I wish this war was over," she wrote:

> Everyone is in continual excitement and fear all the time. My fear is that you will get sick. . . . I dreamed last night you were sick and I started to come to you but I could not get started. I got to the [railroad] cars and they were so full I could hardly get in but I did get a seat and then they were so heavily-loaded they could not run and it seemed as though I could hear you calling me to come to you quick and I woke up crying. You cannot imagine how glad and thankful I was to find it only a dream, still I have felt worried all day for fear something is going to happen but I hope not.

HARPER'S WEEKLY.

A JOURNAL OF CIVILIZATION

Vol. V.—No. 238.] NEW YORK, SATURDAY, JULY 20, 1861. [SINGLE COPIES SIX CENTS. $2.50 PER YEAR IN ADVANCE.

Entered according to Act of Congress, in the Year 1861, by Harper & Brothers, in the Clerk's Office of the District Court for the Southern District of New York.

FILLING CARTRIDGES AT THE UNITED STATES ARSENAL, AT WATERTOWN, MASSACHUSETTS.—[See next Page.]

The start of the Civil War took men, the primary breadwinners in most American families, away from their homes and to the battlefront. Without a steady source of income for their families, many women began working in arsenal factories, replacing male factory workers who either had volunteered for military duty or had been drafted into the army.

Philips's and Thompson's intense fear regarding their loved ones in the military was hardly unusual, as dozens of wartime diaries and letters from the Northern home front reveal. Nor were the women's fears unfounded. "Nearly all civilians would have known someone whose life was in imminent danger," note historians Nelson and Sheriff. "For even though the war saw plenty of quiet spells, rampant disease meant that every soldier was vulnerable at any moment."

With their men's safety a continual concern, Union women waited anxiously for letters from the front. They also became avid newspaper readers, combing local papers for any news regarding their loved ones' regiments. "Contrary to popular wisdom," notes Marilyn Mayer Culpepper in *Trials and Triumphs: The Women of the American Civil War,* " 'no news' did not necessarily signify 'good news.' Reliable reports from the front were often difficult to obtain and mail service could be painfully slow." Consequently, Culpepper writes, "it was sometimes months or even a year before a wife could learn of the fate of her husband or a mother her son." Sarah Chapin, whose husband, Theodore, served with a Michigan volunteer regiment, was tormented by worry when she did not hear from her spouse for a full month after spotting his name on a casualty list that appeared in a Grand Rapids newspaper for the Battle of Murfreesboro in Tennessee. On January 28, 1863, a distraught Sarah wrote to Theodore:

> It is now four weeks since I have heard from you, except an account I have read in the *Eagle* stating that you were wounded at the Battle of Murfreesboro, but not stating how severely. I need not tell you that my anxiety is very great to know where you are and what your circumstances are. And it seems to me sometimes as though I cannot possibly wait much longer without knowing though I am well aware that I may be obliged to wait a great while. . . .

Less than a week later, Chapin finally received the much-awaited letter from her husband, who had been taken to a nearby

Union hospital after the battle. She responded immediately: "I tell you my Dearest one," she wrote,

> it is a heart rending thought to me to know that my dear husband . . . has had so great an amount of suffering to endure in a strange land and with no friendly hand except that of strangers to administer ought to his comfort. I can hardly contain myself at the thought. And it seems to me that I could almost fly until I had reached your couch that I might be with you and take care of you myself. . . . Oh Theodore, if you can only get well enough and they will only let you come home, what a consolation that would be to us all.

Sadly, Sarah Chapin would never see her beloved Theodore again. In June 1863 he died from his wounds in a Nashville hospital, 600 miles (965 km) from their Michigan home.

The Civil War brought death and heartbreak to scores of Northern women like Chapin. For "all their anticipation of tragedy," note Nelson and Sheriff, few "felt prepared when it did arrive." Margaret Scott of Vermont learned of her husband's death at Spotsylvania, Virginia, in May 1864. She was overwhelmed by grief and shock, revealing her anguish in a tearful letter to her sister Harriet:

> I lay in a fainting condition most all night and am so weak in body and mind have pity on me to think he lays on the Battlefield far away without one moments warning and could not send no message to the wife he loved so well. . . . He is dead I never shall see him again Oh I cannot have it so all my hopes in life are oer [over] There is nothing but disappointment and trials in this Wourld. . . .

"The harder part of war is the woman's part," wrote Robert Selph Henry, a well-known Civil War historian of the early twentieth century. Although many people would undoubtedly disagree with Henry's statement, contemporary letters and diaries testify to the agonizing emotional toll that the Civil War took on the hundreds of thousands of women who lost husbands, sons, brothers, and sweethearts in the conflict. "I think the hearts of women suffer more real sorrow than those that are called to still their beating upon the battlefield," wrote one young woman to her soldier fiancée in 1864. The fallen soldiers, she explained, "are at rest and know no more pain; we are left to mourn their loss, and hide our anguish deep in our own hearts."

Southern Women During the Civil War

Like Union propaganda directed at Northern women, Confederate war propaganda urged Southern women to prove their patriotism by encouraging their men to enlist. Government officials publicly praised women who placed loyalty to country above personal concerns regarding male relations. The Southern press frequently ran stories about wives enthusiastically sending their husbands off to whip the Yankees, or belles vowing to end engagements unless their fiancées enlisted. One widely reprinted song from the early days of the war celebrated a fictional heroine who declared that any man who wished to court her "must be a soldier / A veteran from the wars, / One who has fought for 'Southern Rights' / Beneath the Bars and Stars."

In truth, not every Confederate wife, mother, or sweetheart welcomed her loved ones' enlistment, particularly if she did not share the widespread belief among Southerners that the Unionists would quickly lose their will to fight once casualties began to mount. Alabama newlywed Mary Louise Williamson, for example, reported in her private journal that she cried for days when her husband informed her of his intention to enlist in the summer of 1861. On the day of his departure, Williamson admitted in her diary, "This great sorrow makes me forget I ever had such a feeling as patriotism. It seems this war is destined to last a long time. I had no idea it would ever result this seriously."

SUPPORTING THE CONFEDERATE CAUSE AT HOME

Confederate dreams of an easy victory over the Union were to prove short-lived. By early 1862, six months after the First Battle of Bull Run, disease and injuries already had claimed the lives of thousands of Confederate troops. Furthermore, the Union's significant military advantage over the less populous and less industrially developed South was becoming increasingly obvious, even to the most passionate of Confederacy supporters.

Around this time, notes Catherine Clinton in *Tara Revisited: Women, War & the Plantation Legend*, many Southern women's diaries and correspondence started to reflect the kind of misgivings about the war that Mary Williamson had expressed in the summer of 1861. In an emotional letter to her cousin penned in 1862, a South Carolina teen wrote: "Oh! Alice, you cannot be thankful enough that your brothers are not old enough to be soldiers; to be so far away from all that they are near and dear and we know not what time the sad tidings may reach us that they are among those who have fallen among the gallant slain. . . . So very many of my friends have been killed. It makes me sad to think of the past."

Throughout the conflict, hundreds of thousands of women on the Southern home front labored loyally for the Confederate cause. Like their Union counterparts, Confederate women spent countless hours sewing uniforms, knitting scarves and socks, rolling bandages, picking lint, and organizing fund-raisers to provide urgently needed clothing and medical supplies to soldiers on the front. Additionally, in the absence of their male relations, Southern women—and particularly the wives, sisters, and daughters of the region's large planters—were responsible for supplying the bulk of the grains, vegetables, and other food consumed by the Confederate Army during the war. The women's willingness to take on this responsibility was critically important to the military and to the Confederacy's very survival.

The Union's naval forces blockaded major Southern ports during the war. As a result, from mid-1861 onward, most of the Confederacy was cut off from imported goods, including grains and other foodstuffs. This meant farmers and planters, especially those with the most land and slaves, were considered to be vital to the South's wartime strategy. Prior to the war, cotton and other non-food cash crops such as tobacco and indigo (a plant used to make blue dye) had been the core of Southern plantation agriculture. In response to the North's blockade, Confederate officials strongly urged planters to turn over more of their land than ever before to corn, wheat, beans, and other foodstuffs to help feed the Southern fighting force.

Confederate government leaders approved a national military draft in the spring of 1862. With food shortages a constant concern in the blockaded South, it is little wonder that leaders immediately began to worry about how the new draft law would impact how much food Confederate plantations could grow. A few months after the draft went into effect, the Confederate Congress passed a law allowing plantation owners of military age to remain at home for the duration of the war. This law was part of an effort to ensure that food production levels remained stable. The law, which also was intended to protect the South's white population against possible slave rebellions, excused farmers from military service if they oversaw 20 or more slaves.

SOWING AND REAPING.

SOUTHERN WOMEN HOUNDING THEIR MEN ON TO REBELLION.

SOUTHERN WOMEN FEELING THE EFFECTS OF REBELLION, AND CREATING BREAD RIOTS.

As the Civil War continued, many Southern women had to wage their own war of survival at home as Confederate currency declined and families grew hungry. Above, an illustration depicting proud Southern women sending their men off at the beginning of the Civil War and in the 1863 riots, when a shopkeeper refused to lower his prices on flour. The women used hatchets to chop down his door and threatened him until he agreed to sell them the flour at a reduced cost.

At the same time, however, upper-class Southern culture scorned men who avoided military service as dishonorable and cowardly. Because of this attitude, only a tiny minority of those who qualified for the 20-slave rule chose to take advantage of it. Thus, throughout the rural South, planters' female relations were left in charge of family estates. Spurred on by their national and state governments, most plantation mistresses loyally worked to support their side's cause. They abandoned non-food crops such as cotton in order to devote most of their land to the production of grains and vegetables to support the Confederate war effort.

PLANTATION MISTRESSES AND SLAVES

Few female Southerners had any practical business or farming expertise when the war erupted. Because of this, women left in charge of plantations by their male relations often found their new responsibilities intimidating. "Husbands wrote lengthy letters full of agricultural advice about such things as planting,

Middle Class Southern Women Weather the War

During the Civil War, the absence of male breadwinners and sky-high prices for food and other necessities meant that many middle-class Confederate women were forced to find paid work, even though before the conflict virtually no female Southerners of their class had worked outside the home.

Quite a few of them found work during the war as schoolteachers. In the North, a substantial percentage of teachers were female by the mid-1800s. In the pre–Civil War South, however, the teaching profession was overwhelmingly male. For example, right before the war erupted in 1861, just 7 percent of the teachers in the state of North Carolina were female. Yet by the end of the war four years later, fully half were female. Sometimes women had to overcome the strong objections of male relatives in taking teaching positions. The brothers and father of one young Louisiana woman, for instance, were reportedly "much opposed" to her teaching—or working in any job outside of the home. After much heated discussion, "they at last consented that she should do so for a few months." In time, as shown by the enormous growth in the number of female teachers in North Carolina between 1861 and 1865, Southern male "resistance to women in the teaching profession subsided," notes author Marilyn Mayer Culpepper, "and a bright new future for women in the field of education was opened."

harvesting, [and] milking," notes Laura Edwards in *Scarlett Doesn't Live Here Anymore: Southern Women in the Civil War Era.* "But an irregular mail service brought advice sporadically," she observes, so "basically, women were on their own."

What seemed to worry Southern plantation mistresses most during the Civil War, however, was not balancing estate

Like lower-class Confederate women, many middle-class women also found jobs with the Confederate government. However, instead of working for extremely low wages as clothing bureau seamstresses or in dangerous munitions factory jobs, Southern women from more prosperous backgrounds typically found well-paying governmental clerkships. With virtually every able-bodied man in the Confederacy in the army, a variety of governmental agencies including the Post Office, the War Department, and the Quartermaster's Department (which ensured that the Confederate Army was supplied with food, clothing, and equipment) actively sought out female workers.

The single largest employer of women in the Confederate government—as was also the case in the U.S. government—was the Treasury Department. During the course of the war, department officials hired hundreds of women to cut Confederate banknotes and sign them by hand. Aristocratic diarist Mary Boykin Chestnut of South Carolina was shocked to discover among the employees of the Treasury Department not only middle-class Southerners, but also some upper-class women who had fallen on hard financial times. The idea of sheltered Southern ladies venturing out of the "rooftree" of the domestic sphere to toil in public was shameful and unbecoming, she thought. She and another society matron and friend, Mrs. John Preston, vowed that they would rather starve than lower themselves to working at a government office: "Survive or perish—we will not go into one of the departments," Chestnut wrote. "We will not stand up all day and cut notes apart, ordered round by a department clerk. We will live at home with our families and starve in a body. . . . [Treasury] Department—never!"

accounts or deciding which crops to plant. Rather, it was how to control their families' numerous slaves. Although plantation mistresses traditionally supervised household slaves, the vast majority had no experience overseeing large gangs of field workers. As their wartime letters and diaries reveal, many of the women felt deeply ill equipped and vulnerable in their new role as slave managers.

Judging by their writings, these women's concerns about being able to manage slaves focused mostly on one issue: the willingness of slaves to take orders from a woman when they were not used to female authority. "Master's eye and voice are much more potent [powerful] than mistress', " Mrs. Catherine Ann Edmondston of North Carolina fretted early in the war. Virginian Ellen Moore, another planter's wife left to manage on her own during the war, was convinced that her field slaves were slacking off because "all think I am a kind of usurper [someone who grabs power from someone else] & have no authority over them."

Yet the fears that many plantation mistresses harbored regarding their ability to control their slaves ran deeper than their concerns about the slaves' productivity in the fields. Before the Civil War, slaves were thought of as loyal, gentle, and even childlike. When the war erupted, however, many white Southerners finally began to face the truth regarding their culture's self-serving myths about slaves. Across the South, lone plantation mistresses worried that their slaves would rise up violently against them, inspired by the war and the dreams of freedom it promised. Keziah Brevard of South Carolina, for instance, admitted to being terrified of her slave force of 200. "It is dreadful to dwell on insurrections [rebellions]. Yet many an hour have I laid awake . . . thinking of our danger," she wrote in 1861. That same year a widowed plantation mistress in Louisiana fretted to her sister: "Can we cope with an enemy abroad & one at home—Negroes are fully alive to the state of things. . . . I can imagine all sorts of noises at night and sometimes think they are right at my door."

CONFRONTING HUNGER AND DESPAIR

Only about 30 percent of the whites in the South were slave-holders. This meant that the vast majority of rural Confederate women had no need to worry about rebellious slaves. They had plenty else to worry about, however. With their male relations off at war, Southern farmwomen were often solely responsible for planting, tending, and harvesting their crops in addition to their regular childcare and other domestic duties.

Many Northern farmwives also had to provide for them-selves and their families by toiling in the fields during the war. Yet the economic and physical hardships that rural women in the South faced were truly oppressive. As the war dragged on, they faced government seizures of food crops, farming equip-ment, and livestock for the Confederate armed forces; pillag-ing and destruction of property by invading Union troops; widespread food and clothing shortages; and out-of-control inflation. Moreover, a far higher percentage of Southern than Northern wives and daughters were left without their male breadwinners during the Civil War. Fully 4 out of 5 white men of military age volunteered for or were drafted into the Con-federate Army during the conflict. In the more populous North about 2 out of 5 eligible men served in the military. Adding to the woes of Southern women, a significantly higher percentage of Confederate than Union soldiers never returned home at all from the war. According to some estimates, 20 percent of the adult white male population in the South died in the war, while just over 5 percent of the North's adult white male population perished.

In some parts of the South, droughts and meager harvests made the economic plight of poorer rural families so desperate that wives were reduced to pleading with their soldier husbands to desert. After describing her long and unsuccessful struggle to provide her family with even the barest essentials of life, a Virginia farm wife wrote to her husband in the Confederate

Army: "We having nothing in the house to eat but a little bit of meal [coarsely ground corn or other grain]." If he did not return home soon to her and the children, she warned, " 'twant be no use to come, for we'll . . . be out there . . . in the old grave yard with your ma and pa."

Other women, rather than trying to persuade their spouses to desert, abandoned the countryside for nearby cities and towns. Thousands of impoverished farm wives took this road in hopes of securing a paying job in a shop or factory. Quite a few managed to eke out modest livings as seamstresses for the Confederate Clothing Bureau, which furnished uniforms and other clothing to soldiers. Others toiled in government munitions plants, a hazardous business—nearly 50 women were killed in an 1863 explosion in a Richmond arsenal, for example. Despite the danger, the wages were almost as tiny as those offered by the clothing bureau. By 1863, shortages and runaway inflation had caused prices of dietary staples such as butter, potatoes, and flour to increase tenfold from what they had been just three years earlier. Many urban female wage earners were finding it harder and harder to feed themselves and their children.

From the spring of 1863 until the war's end two years later, the frustration of working-class women with high food prices erupted into rioting in cities across the South, including Atlanta, Savannah, and Macon, Georgia; Mobile, Alabama; and Petersburg, Virginia. Popularly known as "Bread Riots," the female-led protests usually began as peaceful demonstrations to demand government assistance for hungry families but soon degenerated into widespread looting of stores and warehouses for bread, meat, and other staples. The most famous of the Southern Bread Riots occurred in the Confederate capital of Richmond on April 2, 1863, when hundreds of women, many of them armed with hatchets or knives, ransacked local shops and government warehouses for food. As one young rioter explained to a shocked bystander, the loaves of bread and other food that she and her fellow looters stole were "little enough for the government to give us after it has taken all our men." Not until more than a dozen stores and warehouses had been stripped bare was the disturbance finally brought under control.

REBEL WOMEN AND NORTHERN SOLDIERS IN OCCUPIED TERRITORIES

Few Northern women ever came face to face with a Confederate soldier during the Civil War. In sharp contrast, large numbers of Southern women came into contact with Union troops, and many lived for long periods of time under their occupation. For example, Nashville, Tennessee, and the South's largest city, New Orleans, both fell to Union forces in early 1862. The two cities would remain under direct Union military control for the final three years of the Civil War.

The hostility of Confederate women in occupied territories toward their Union conquerors is legendary. Nowhere did they treat Northern troops with more hatred than they did in New Orleans. To show their disdain for the bluecoats, females of all ages and classes haughtily flounced out of public rooms and off streetcars whenever soldiers entered, made rude comments as they passed by, and even spat or swore at them. At first the Union soldiers tried to be gentlemen and ignored the women's insulting words and behavior. But within a month of the Union takeover of New Orleans, the city's top administrator, General Benjamin Butler, decided that he had had enough.

In May 1862, after a well-known New Orleans society woman went so far as to dump the contents of a full chamber pot from a balcony onto the head of a Union officer, Butler issued his infamous General Order, No. 28, also known as the "Woman's Order." In the order Butler declared that any female in the city who "show[ed] contempt for any officer or private of the United States" would be "regarded and held liable to be treated as a woman of the town plying her vocation" (in other words, treated like a prostitute). If the city's supposedly proper

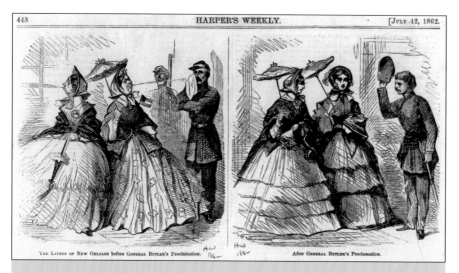

448   HARPER'S WEEKLY.   [July 12, 1862.

The Ladies of New Orleans before General Butler's Proclamation.   After General Butler's Proclamation.

Southern women in occupied territories did their best to make Federal troops feel unwelcome. A small group even turned their backsides toward General Benjamin Butler, causing him to remark, "These women evidently know which end of them looks the best." Manners improved under Butler's "Woman's Order." Above, an illustration showing Southern women spitting on Union troops before Butler's proclamation and their reformed behavior afterward.

and polite ladies chose to conduct themselves with the vulgarity of a common prostitute, Butler reasoned, then they should expect to be treated like one.

General Order, No. 28 generated widespread anger throughout the South as "an assault on female purity," notes Drew Gilpin Faust in *Mothers of Invention: Women of the Slaveholding South in the American Civil War*. Even so, the controversial measure proved quite effective. "The fear of being perceived as a 'woman of the town' was so great, the threatened loss of honor so unthinkable" for New Orleans's female population, writes Faust, "that no Yankee officer was ever faced with actually carrying out the order's threat."

Despite the deep hostility that many Confederate women showed toward the Northern occupying troops, a sizable number of Southern women in occupied areas actually ended up marrying Union soldiers during or soon after the war. One Nashville teenager complained in a letter to her brother that with most of the local boys gone at war, many of the city's most eligible belles were "dropping off into the arms of the ruthless invader." Among these female turncoats, she noted with scorn, was one who had once slept "with the Bonnie Blue Flag [a popular symbol of Southern independence] under her pillow." In Natchez, Mississippi, which fell to Union troops in 1863, young Southerner Kate Foster also was upset by the budding romances between several local girls and Northern soldiers: "Some of the young ladies around Natchez are receiving attention from the

"What . . . Will Become of Us Poor Women and Children?"

In 1864 an anonymous woman from rural North Carolina, struggling to feed her family following the death of her husband in combat, wrote in desperation to her state's chief executive, Governor Zebulon B. Vance. She pleaded with him to try to end what she called "this cruel war." Filled with spelling and grammatical errors and nearly illegible in places, the letter is a heartbreaking reminder of the enormous hardships endured by poor Southern women during the Civil War:

> Especly for they sake of sufering women and children do try and stop this cruel war. Her I am without one mouthfull to eat myself and five children and God only knows where I will get somthin, now you know . . . that it is imposible to whip they yankees, therefor I beg you for God sake to try and make peace on some terms and let they rest of they poor men come home and try to make something to eat, my husband has ben kiled, and if they all stay till they are dead, what in they name of God will become of us poor women and children?

Yankees," Kate confided in her diary. "I think it shows *so* little character not to resist love of admiration more," she sniffed.

Perhaps no union involving a bluecoat and a Southerner generated more bad feeling than that between Eleanor Swain, the daughter of University of North Carolina President David Swain, and Union General Richard Atkins. "North Carolinians were infuriated when the engagement was announced," notes Mary Elizabeth Massey. Even a decade after the wedding, a friend of the Swains reported, some North Carolinians had "not yet forgiven" Eleanor for stooping so low as to marry "a Yankee."

WHEN HOME FRONT AND BATTLEFRONT MERGE

The Confederate states were the scene of virtually all of the fighting during the war. In the South, notes author Marilyn Mayer Culpepper, "the Civil War was notorious for its upheaval of families, principally those comprised of lone women and children." From 1862 on, as the Union advanced ever farther into the South, tens of thousands of women in the troops' path hastily packed up their children and whatever household items they could gather and headed for safer locations. Uncertainty and hardship were the situation of most of the refugees, some of whom ended up moving five or six times in the search for a place to stay. The most fortunate ones found temporary homes with sympathetic relatives, friends, or acquaintances. Many others were reduced to living in abandoned buildings, caves, or any other shelter they could find.

Although the majority of Southern refugees left their homes voluntarily, thousands were forcibly evacuated. In some cases they were removed by their own army, which frequently took over private residences to use as officers' quarters or hospitals. Numerous others were driven out by enemy troops, as was the case in Atlanta on September 4, 1864. After conquering Atlanta, the main Confederate commercial and transportation center, General William Tecumseh Sherman ordered its mostly female population out of the city. "With few exceptions the noncombatants were hustled out of Atlanta," writes Mary Elizabeth Massey, "including some aged, infirm women and some in the throes of childbirth. They were dumped in Macon [about 80 miles, or 130 km, south of Atlanta] where they lived crowded together in boxcars, tents, or camps in the open country, for the city was unable to accommodate them." (Boxcars are enclosed railroad cars used to transport goods.)

Two months after taking Atlanta, Sherman and his 62,000-man force set off on their famous "March to the Sea." They pushed southeastward through Georgia to the port city of Savannah, where they arrived just before Christmas. The following month Sherman led his troops back northward through South Carolina and North Carolina toward Richmond to join up with the forces of Union General-in-Chief Ulysses Grant. In both the Georgia and the Carolinas campaign, Sherman commanded his army to live off the countryside. This harsh tactic was meant to break the spirits of the Southern people by demonstrating that their leadership could not protect them or their property from the might of the U.S. government.

As Sherman led his troops through Georgia and the Carolinas in late 1864 and early 1865, foragers—or "bummers" as they were dubbed—were sent out in all directions from the main force to gather food and fuel for the army. Sherman commanded the bummers to refrain from needlessly destroying civilian property or taking anything that was not needed for the army's survival. Nonetheless, according to the journals and memoirs of Southern women who lived along the general's path, many of the foragers ignored Sherman's orders. Fueled by greed or a desire for revenge, they stole valuables and household goods as well as food and firewood from Southern families. They also vandalized or torched scores of farm fields, outbuildings, and houses.

Since the vast majority of Southern men of military age were in the army, women in Georgia and the Carolinas found

Thousands of Southerners voluntarily left or were forced to leave their homes by Union forces. Many of those who stayed witnessed Federal troops plunder and destroy their stored food, fields, and homes. Although this was the end of an era for the South, it also became a new beginning for freed slaves. U.S. painter and politician George Caleb Bingham created the painting "Martial Law" (above) to illustrate the painful and dramatic upheaval of forced evacuation under Federal troops in Missouri.

themselves confronting Sherman's dreaded bummers on their own. There was little they could do to stop the plundering and vandalism, as Dolly Lunt Burge of Covington, Georgia, quickly discovered. "But like demons they rush in!" she moaned in her diary when Union foragers swooped down on her plantation. "My yards are full. To my smoke house, my dairy, pantry, kitchen, and cellar, like famished wolves they come, breaking locks and whatever is in their way. . . . Utterly powerless I ran out and appealed to the guard. 'I cannot help you, Madam: it is orders.' "

Sherman's troops captured Columbia, the capital of South Carolina, in February 1865. Louisa McCord Smythe, who was living with four female relatives in one of the city's wealthier neighborhoods, described her shock and terror when Union looters suddenly charged into her backyard:

> Without any warning our back gate was burst violently open and in rushed pell mell, crowding, pushing, almost falling over each other, such a crowd of men as I never saw before or since. They seemed scarcely human in their fierce excitement—the excitement of greed and rapine [plunder]. In one instant the large yard was full of them. . . . They robbed even the Negroes. What they couldn't take they spoiled. I didn't actually see it done but in many places they ripped up feather beds, poured molasses over the feathers and threw the whole into the wells! . . . In a few minutes the ground was honeycombed with stabs from bayonets as these wild creatures rushed around prodding the earth in search of buried treasures—we stood petrified and fascinated at the window watching.

For Smythe and hundreds of thousands of other white Southern women, the arrival of the Yankee invaders meant terror and the specter of defeat. For enslaved black women, however, the appearance of Union troops on Southern soil signified something quite different: a long-awaited opportunity for freedom and a better life for themselves and their loved ones.

African-American Women During the Civil War

Historians' knowledge of the experiences and contributions of female African Americans during the Civil War has been severely limited. This is due to the fact that, to date, few firsthand accounts of the war by black women have been uncovered. Because it was against the law to teach slaves to read and write in the pre-war South, a much smaller number of black than white women left behind wartime diaries, letters, or other writings. The only Civil War memoir by an African-American woman to be published was Susie King Taylor's *Reminiscences of My Life in Camp with the 33rd United States Colored Troops.* Her memoir stressed the critical yet largely unnoticed role that women of color played in the conflict, particularly in aiding the Union Army. Taylor was a former slave who served as a laundress and nurse with an all-black Union regiment for nearly the entire war. In the introduction to her wartime narrative, she noted:

> There are many people who do not know what some of the colored women did during the war. There were hundreds

98

of them who assisted the Union soldiers by hiding them and helping them to escape. Many were punished for taking food to the prison stockades for the prisoners. . . . Others assisted in various ways the Union army. These things should be kept in history before the people. There has never been a greater war in the United States than the one of 1861, where so many lives were lost—not men alone but noble women as well.

One African-American woman who has received widespread recognition for her wartime contributions over the years is the celebrated heroine of the Underground Railroad and arguably the best-known black woman in U.S. history: Harriet Tubman.

HARRIET TUBMAN AND THE UNION CAUSE

During the decade leading up to the Civil War, Harriet Tubman established a reputation as the most successful "conductor," or guide, on the Underground Railroad, the secret interracial network that helped runaway slaves escape from the South. Tubman was the secret liberty line's first—and according to some historians, only—female conductor. She shepherded at least 200 runaway slaves from Maryland, Virginia, and Delaware to safety in Canada or the free states of the North between 1850 and 1861.

Born into slavery in about 1820, Tubman fled her owner's Maryland plantation for Pennsylvania in 1849 after hearing rumors that she was about to be sold away from her family to out-of-state buyers. Convinced that God had personally called her to protect and uplift her downtrodden people, within a year of her escape Tubman was back in the South, courageously risking her own hard-earned liberty so that other African Americans could secure theirs.

Like most Americans who opposed slavery, Tubman welcomed the Civil War. President Lincoln was anxious to keep the

Harriet Tubman was one of the most well-known female figures of the Civil War era. Known to many as "Moses," she helped slaves escape from the South and into the North to freedom. When the fighting began, she was quick to volunteer her services to the Union cause and worked as a nurse and a spy, and even led a daring undercover military operation behind Confederate lines.

slaveholding border states of Missouri, Kentucky, and Maryland from leaving the Union. Thus, for nearly the first two years of the conflict, he had been careful to portray the war solely as a struggle to preserve the Union and not as an attack on slavery. Even the president's famous Emancipation Proclamation of January 1863 was designed to calm the border states by only freeing slaves in the rebellious Confederate states and not in those slaveholding states that remained loyal to the Union.

Despite Lincoln's hesitancy to link the Union war effort too closely with the antislavery cause, from the very start of the fighting Tubman and other black abolitionists were confident that a Union victory would lead to slavery's demise throughout the United States. Consequently, when the war broke out in April 1861, Tubman immediately offered her services to the Union. A few months later, the army sent her to the Union-occupied Sea Islands near Charleston to provide humanitarian assistance to black refugees from the area's vast cotton plantations. Her chief assignment was to act as a Union spy and scout behind Confederate lines. When the Emancipation Proclamation finally allowed the Union Army to accept black soldiers in January 1863, Tubman also helped the Union recruit five African-American regiments on the Sea Islands. The principal duty of the all-black units was to carry out raiding missions on the nearby South Carolina mainland to take away slaves and other valuable enemy "property." In recognition of her exceptional daring and resourcefulness as a scout, spy, and Underground Railroad conductor, Tubman was given a central role in planning and executing the undercover military operations.

The most successful and famous military expedition that Tubman helped direct in the South Carolina interior was the Combahee River Raid of 1863. On the night of June 2, Tubman led three gunboats filled with African-American troops from the Sea Islands to Confederate warehouses and ammunition stockpiles near the Combahee River. They continued on to link up with hundreds of runaway slaves whom she had secretly

Sojourner Truth

After Harriet Tubman, the most famous African-American woman of the Civil War was Sojourner Truth. Like Tubman, Truth was a former slave and devoted abolitionist. Christened Isabella Baumfree, she was born in rural New York in about 1797, when slavery was still legal in that state. In 1826, shortly before slavery was finally abolished in New York, she ran away from her abusive master. Settling in New York City, Baumfree became a popular preacher and took the name of Sojourner Truth to highlight what she believed to be her divine mission: to *sojourn*, or travel, through the United States teaching God's truth. A charismatic orator, she lectured on her Christian beliefs, the evils of slavery, and women's rights in dozens of Northern towns and cities during the decades before the Civil War.

Early in the Civil War, Truth pressed the U.S. government to allow African Americans to serve in the Union Army. Once blacks finally were allowed to enlist in January 1863, she tirelessly collected food, clothing, and other essential supplies for their regiments. Truth also worked for better conditions for freed slaves living in refugee camps, including the huge Freedman's Village, located just outside Washington, D.C. In 1864 she was appointed to the national Freedman's Relief Association and was invited by President Lincoln to speak with him at the White House. Truth was a firm supporter of women's suffrage, and she befriended white women's rights leaders Susan B. Anthony and Elizabeth Cady Stanton during the war. (She was dismayed, however, when Stanton threatened to withdraw her support for African-American suffrage unless women were given the vote at the same time.) Until her death on November 26, 1883, Truth continued to speak out on her three favorite subjects: her Christian faith, equal political and economic opportunities for African Americans, and women's rights.

instructed to hide along the riverbank. As a result of her skillful planning and leadership, the Union raiders were able to plunder hundreds of thousands of dollars worth of Confederate commissary stores, cotton, and property, and make off with nearly 800 field slaves, all without suffering a single casualty. When Northern journalists discovered that a woman—and a former slave at that—had helped to direct a major military raid into Confederate territory, they were intrigued and gave the story extensive newspaper coverage.

After the Combahee Raid, Tubman remained on the Sea Islands for another year, continuing her undercover work as a scout and spy and providing medical care to the troops stationed there. In 1865 she headed for Fort Monroe, Virginia, where she put in long hours as a nurse at several army hospitals, including at a severely understaffed facility for African-American soldiers.

Despite Tubman's many contributions to the Union war effort, by the conflict's end the U.S. Army had paid her just $200 in wages. With the backing of several high-ranking military and civilian officials, Tubman petitioned Congress after the war for her lost back-pay and for a veteran's pension, with no success. "You wouldn't think that after I served the flag so faithfully I should come to want under its folds," she complained bitterly to a friend. When Tubman died virtually penniless in Auburn, New York, in 1913, the army finally awarded the heroine of the Combahee River Raid belated recognition for her tireless and courageous assistance to the Union by providing her with a full military burial.

AFRICAN-AMERICAN WOMEN OF THE SOUTH AND THE UNION ARMY

Aside from Harriet Tubman, several other escaped female slaves also are known to have provided vital military assistance to the Union cause. They included light-skinned Maria Lewis, who disguised herself as a white man and fought on the frontlines with the 8th New York Cavalry, and Lucy Carter, who spied for the Union Army in Virginia. Mary Louveste, a free black woman who lived near the Gosport Navy Yard in Norfolk, Virginia, also served as a Union spy. Louveste personally passed along critical information regarding Confederate naval vessels to Gideon Welles, secretary of the U.S. Navy. "Mrs. Louveste encountered no small risk in bringing this information," Welles later wrote. "I am aware of none more meritorious than this poor colored woman whose zeal and fidelity I remember and acknowledge with gratitude."

Despite being classified as "regimental laundress," Susie King Taylor, the author of the only published Civil War memoir by an African-American woman, served in a variety of positions with the 33rd U.S. Colored Infantry in South Carolina, Georgia, and Florida for most of the war. Among other duties, the former slave took apart, cleaned, and tested the soldiers' guns and nursed the regiment's ill and wounded. She also offered instruction in reading and writing to any men who were interested in acquiring those skills. Taylor had fled her owners in Savannah, Georgia, in 1862 at age 14 to seek sanctuary behind Union lines. She had been secretly taught to read and write as a child by white playmates in direct opposition to the laws of her home state.

Taylor was just one of thousands of female slaves who sought protection in the Union Army in the South during the war. Many female "contrabands," as the runaways were commonly known, ended up working for the Union military as laundresses, nurses, or cooks. Their payment most often came in the form of daily soldier's rations rather than cash wages. The Union pressed others into hard physical labor. Assigned to work in gangs along with male fugitives, the women helped construct battlements and dig ditches—tasks that white officers never would have ordered a vivandière or any other white woman attached to the military to undertake. Many Union

"Dabney's Wife": One of the War's Most Creative Spies

An African-American female slave escaped with her husband to General Joseph Hooker's headquarters camp on the Northern bank of Virginia's Rappahannock River in early 1863. An officer in Hooker's camp later recorded the exploits of the woman, whom he called "Dabney's wife" (her first name is lost to history).

The female runaway soon disappeared again behind Confederate lines, while her husband stayed behind with the Union troops. As it turned out, Mrs. Dabney was not switching her loyalty: Rather, she had decided to attach herself to the Confederate camp on the Southern side of the Rappahannock as a laundress and cook in order to spy for the Union. Mrs. Dabney would quietly observe Confederate troop movements, then relay the information back to the Union Army through her husband.

Her method of sending information to Mr. Dabney was very clever: She used the clothesline on which she dried the soldiers' laundry as a sort of telegraph. The Union officer recorded her husband's explanation of the secret clothesline signal system in his account of the female-runaway-turned-federal-spy:

> That clothes-line tells me in half an hour just what goes on at [General Robert E.] Lee's headquarters. You see my wife over there; she washes for the officers, and cooks, and waits around, and as soon as she hears about any movement or anything going on, she comes down and moves the clothes on that line so I can understand in a minute. That there gray shirt is [General James] Longstreet; and when she takes it off, it means he's gone down about Richmond. The white shirt means [General Ambrose P.] Hill; and when she moves it up to the west end of the line, Hill's corp has moved up stream. The red one is [General] Stonewall [Jackson]. He's down on the right now, and if he moves, she will move that red shirt.

officers were only too happy to take advantage of the cheap labor that escaped female slaves provided. Others struggled to keep the women out of their camps. General Grenville Dodge, for instance, was dismayed by how many of the female runaways who sought refuge with his troops in Alabama brought small children with them. This made it difficult, if not impossible, for them to work in exchange for their rations. Because the mothers and their young dependents consumed food and other essential supplies without giving anything back to the unit, they "are a burden to us and should stay on the plantations," Dodge declared unsympathetically.

BLACK WOMEN WHO REMAINED ENSLAVED DURING THE WAR

For every female slave who fled her plantation to seek refuge with the Union troops, many more remained behind. The vast majority of female slaves would not attain their freedom until after the surrender of the Confederate Army at Appomattox Courthouse on April 9, 1865. Most of the enslaved women who chose to stay put during the war probably were motivated by fear. If recaptured, runaway slaves faced brutal punishments, including mutilation, branding, floggings, and even death. One Kentucky slave later described how her attempt to flee for Union lines with her seven-year-old child was quickly foiled by her master's cruel son-in-law, "who told me that if I did not go back with him he would shoot me. He drew a pistol on me as he made this threat. I could offer no resistance as he constantly kept the pistol pointed at me." After escorting her home at gunpoint, the son-in-law informed the terrified woman that he would be keeping her child as a hostage in his own home to discourage any future escape attempts on her part.

Most female slaves decided that remaining where they were was the safest course of action for themselves and for their children. As the war ground on, however, life on the plantations became ever more difficult for slaves. During the conflict, everyone in the Confederacy suffered from extremely high prices and shortages of food, clothing, and other necessities. Yet no single group in the South was harder hit by these economic hardships than the region's enslaved population. "Slaveholders gave low priority to slaves' needs," notes historian Laura Edwards. "It was not unusual to see barefooted, half-naked slaves working the fields during the war. Hunger was equally common. In 1862, several planters on the South Carolina coast eliminated everything but rice from their slaves' rations." Two years later, Missouri slave Ann Valentine wrote to her husband, Andrew, a free black serving in the 2nd Missouri Colored Infantry of the Union Army: "You do not know how bad I am treated. They [her slave owners] are treating me worse every day. Our child cries for you. Send me some money as soon as you can for me and my child are almost naked."

Female slaves during the war also were forced to cope with a significantly increased workload as replacements for absent male field slaves. A number of the absent men had been forced into service by the Confederate government to build fortifications or toil in other military projects. Nearly 100,000 others fled their plantations to enlist in the Union Army once the Union began accepting black soldiers in January 1863. The Union blockade made manufactured cloth virtually impossible to obtain in the South at the same time that female slaves were putting in longer days than ever before in the fields. Because of this, many female slaves were forced to toil well into the night spinning and weaving homemade cloth for their owners' households.

While the war brought numerous hardships to enslaved women, it also gave them new reason for hope. As Union troops advanced into Southern territory, many female slaves were emboldened to oppose their masters' authority by working more slowly or refusing to perform certain plantation duties altogether. Others daringly aided Union soldiers who had become lost, ill, or injured. "Many a soldier will remember how, when he fell out of the ranks during one of those severe marches, and the planter nearby scowled and glowered so that he could not enter the rich man's door," some sympathetic slave woman "helped him to her own cabin, . . . made him tea and gruel, and nursed him as tenderly as his sister would have done," one white Union soldier recalled in his Civil War memoirs. Another appreciative Union soldier described in his wartime diary how local slave women courageously assisted him and other escapees from a Confederate prison camp in South Carolina: "Still in the woods, the women coming to us twice during the day to bring us food and inform us that a guide will be ready at dark. God bless the poor slaves."

"FOR THE BENEFIT OF THE SUFFERING BLACKS"

From 1862 on, as Northern troops pushed ever farther into the South and more and more slaves fled to Union lines, thousands of the escapees were herded into makeshift Union refugee camps. In the poorly organized and crowded camps, the refugees died in shockingly high numbers from malnutrition, infectious disease, and exposure. When reports of the camps' horrendous conditions reached the North's free black community, there was an outpouring of sympathy and aid for the former slaves, particularly among the community's female members. In order to obtain funds to purchase sorely needed medical supplies, food, and clothing for the refugees, the women created new charitable organizations. They also widened the missions of black charitable societies that were already established.

One of the best known and most successful of the black female fund-raisers of the Civil War era was former slave Elizabeth Keckly of Washington, D.C. Keckly had purchased her freedom from her Missouri owner five years before the war's outbreak. She was a highly skilled seamstress whose many socially elite clients included President Lincoln's wife, Mary Todd Lincoln. In August 1862, Keckly took time from her busy dressmaking business to establish a national black women's aid society, the Contraband Relief Association (CRA). The following year she published an editorial in a popular African-American newspaper calling for Northern blacks, and particularly middle-class ones such as herself, to rally behind the desperately poor refugees. Free blacks of means, she asserted, had a pressing moral responsibility:

> . . . to do all we can to assist . . . those whose lot has hitherto been cast in the dark, rough paths of life. . . . If the white people can give festivals to raise funds for the relief of suffering soldiers, why should not the well-to-do colored people go to work to do something for the benefit of the suffering blacks. . . . Who, in appearing before the Great Judge when life is over, would not rejoice to have done what he could for those destitute brothers and sisters?

In addition to raising money to assist the contrabands, Northern black women labored directly among the former slaves as relief workers or nurses, and occasionally as teachers. During the war nearly 1,000 Northerners, three-quarters of them female, set up makeshift schools and instructed refugees of all ages in reading, writing, and arithmetic. They worked under the guidance of the American Missionary Association and a variety of other religious and charitable organizations. The vast majority of the instructors hired by the American Missionary Association and the other major Northern aid organizations were white, but a number of African-American women also served as teachers in the occupied South. One of the first African-American teachers to head to the South during the war was a young middle-class woman from Philadelphia named Charlotte Forten.

Forten was born in Philadelphia in 1837 into a prosperous black family with strong ties to the abolitionist movement. As a teenager, Forten attended Salem Normal School in Massachu-setts, one of the few teacher's colleges in the nineteenth-century United States that admitted students of different races. On re-ceiving her teacher's certificate in 1856, Forten taught at a Salem grammar school that permitted both white and black students. This made her the first African-American teacher in the city to instruct white students. After the Union Army conquered the South Carolina Sea Islands in late 1861, dozens of instructors from Massachusetts and elsewhere in the North were recruited to teach the islands' newly freed slaves. Convinced that educa-tion was critical to the advancement of the African-American people, Forten decided in 1862 to apply for a position with a Northern relief organization that sponsored teachers on the occupied islands. Although her application was turned down—seemingly because of her race—Forten was persistent and soon found a Philadelphia-based missionary group that was willing to sponsor her.

Because of her own experiences with racial discrimination in the North, Forten was determined to plant a sense of racial pride and solidarity in her South Carolina students. In Novem-ber 1862, she noted in her diary that she had lectured her pupils about "the noble Toussaint," meaning Toussaint L'Ouverture, a black slave in Haiti who had led a successful revolt against the Caribbean island's white rulers six decades earlier. "They listened very attentively," she noted. "It is well that they should know what one of their own color could do for his race. I long to inspire them with courage and ambition (of a noble sort), and high purpose." Forten took enormous satisfaction from her students' thirst for knowledge and academic accomplish-ments, particularly in view of the widespread belief among white Americans that people of African descent were intellec-tually inferior to whites. "I find the children . . . eager to learn, and many make most rapid improvement," she noted in 1864 in an article for the *Atlantic Monthly* chronicling her experi-ences on the Sea Islands. "It is a great happiness to teach them.

Although many female slaves fled their plantations to seek sanctuary with Union troops during the Civil War, the majority chose to remain behind. Life on the plantations became increasingly difficult for them as the war ground on. Not only were food and other basic necessities in short supply on most plantations, but female slaves had to take on additional work in the fields as more and more male slaves joined the Union Army or were forced into service by the Confederate government.

I wish some of those persons at the North, who say the race is hopelessly and naturally inferior, could see the readiness with which these children, so long oppressed and deprived of every privilege, learn and understand." Forten spent nearly two years on the Sea Islands before ill health caused her to return home to Pennsylvania.

BLACK WOMEN AND SOLDIERS' AID SOCIETIES

Beginning in early 1863 when African Americans finally were permitted to serve in the Union Army, Northern black women focused their relief efforts on aiding black soldiers as well as escaped slaves. "Given the climate of racial hostility which existed in the country," notes historian Ella Forbes in *African American Women During the Civil War*, "African-American soldiers' relief associations were, no doubt, established because of the fear and likelihood that white sanitary relief societies would not extend courtesies to black soldiers." Like white soldiers' aid societies, the Colored Women's Sanitary Commission of Philadelphia and other black women's groups raised money to purchase essential supplies for the troops; sewed and knitted uniforms, scarves, and other clothing for the men; rolled bandages; and nursed the ill and wounded. Their work was critically important to the physical well-being of the soldiers they served, since the U.S. Army routinely provided African-American units with lower quality clothing, food, and medical care than white units.

Many African-American women who participated in soldier relief efforts were clearly inspired by the belief that their work promoted not only the best interests of the black troops, but of black Americans as a whole. "More than simply aiding specific soldiers," argues historian Nina Silber, "black women tended to see their work as a way of advancing the cause of emancipation and the standing of the race." Louisa Jacobs was a leader in black relief efforts for African-American troops in the North. Jacobs's words regarding the enlisted men she and her fellow female volunteers sought to help lend support to Silber's claim:

Their cause is our cause. By their suffering and death our recognition as a people widens. . . . I rejoice that the nation was forced at last to accept the assistance from the men, who, in the beginning of the rebellion, forgetting the wrongs of a life-time, proffered their services to the country. Their patriotism was scorned; but as the storm of war went on, the strength of their arms became a necessity. . . . With pride we can point to the fact, that he who was least among men, became a potent help in their dark hour of need.

RACIAL AND GENDER EQUALITY

Between 1863 and 1865, nearly 200,000 African Americans fought to end slavery and save the Union in the nation's "dark hour of need." Their sacrifice was great: Nearly 40,000 men—1 in every 5 black enlisted men—would lose their lives to illness or battlefield injuries during the Civil War. The passage in January 1865 of the Thirteenth Amendment, which declared racial slavery unconstitutional, and the surrender of the Confederate forces four months later finally brought an end to legalized human bondage throughout the United States. Yet, as historian Laura Edwards points out, for the country's black population, "destroying slavery . . . would prove far easier than establishing freedom." African-American men's and women's struggle to be treated as full and equal citizens of the United States began during the war and would continue for many generations to come after the Confederate surrender at Appomattox Courthouse in April 1865.

During the years following the Civil War, the struggle to achieve gender equality in the United States also would prove to be a slow and frustrating process, despite the vital contributions American women made to the war effort and the new economic and social roles many took on during the conflict. Although the widespread use of female nurses in the Civil War did allow women to secure a permanent place in the nursing profession during the postwar era, most of the gains that women made in other occupations and fields during the conflict would prove temporary.

Some prominent female activists such as Susan B. Anthony and Harriet Tubman were inspired by their wartime experiences to press harder than ever before for political and legal equality for women. The majority of American women, however, were not yet ready to embrace feminism during the years immediately after the war. Instead, in the wake of the terrible upheavals and devastation of the conflict, most appeared content to retreat to their traditional prewar sphere: the private world of home and family. The feminist movement would not gain widespread support in the United States until the beginning of the twentieth century. Women finally won the right to vote in national elections in 1920, more than a half-century after the Civil War came to an end.

Glossary

ABOLITIONIST An individual who wants to abolish or do away with slavery.

ARSENAL A place where ammunition and other military materials are produced or stored.

BLOCKADE An effort to weaken an enemy's economy by preventing all ships—including trading vessels—from leaving or entering its ports.

BORDER STATES Missouri, Maryland, and Kentucky, all of which contained substantial numbers of slaveholders in 1861, yet remained within the Union; they were referred to as "border states" during the Civil War because of their location along the border between the Confederacy and the North.

BOXCAR An enclosed railroad car used to transport goods.

BUMMERS Soldiers assigned to act as foragers for General William T. Sherman's Union forces as they marched through Georgia and the Carolinas in late 1864 and early 1865.

CALICO A coarse, brightly printed cotton cloth often used in making women's clothing during the nineteenth century.

CAVALRY Soldiers who traveled and fought on horseback.

COMPANY Led by a captain, during the Civil War era a company was usually made up of 100 soldiers.

CONFEDERACY Also known as the South, the Confederacy, or the Confederate States of America; included the 11 states that seceded from the Union between December 1860 and April 1861 to form their own independent nation: South and North Carolina, Texas,

Mississippi, Florida, Alabama, Georgia, Louisiana, Tennessee, Arkansas, and Virginia.

CONTRABAND   A name commonly given to a runaway slave who fled to Union lines.

FEDERALS   Another name for members of the Union armed forces.

HACK   A hired coach.

HARDTACK   A dry biscuit made with only water and flour.

HOOPS   Fashionable during the decade before the Civil War, hoops were lightweight circular frames that were used to make a woman's skirt fuller.

INDIGO   A plant whose berries were used to make a popular blue dye.

INFANTRY SOLDIER   A soldier who traveled and fought on foot.

INFLATION   An increase in the price of goods and services.

LINT   A soft material created by scraping old cotton or other fabric with a knife to be used in packing wounds.

MILLWRIGHT   A workman who made or repaired machinery used in a mill.

RATION   A fixed portion of food given out to persons in military service.

REGIMENT   Typically made up of 1,000 to 1,500 soldiers, the regiment was the basic military unit of the Civil War.

SABOTAGE   The deliberate destruction of property or slowing down of normal operations by civilians or undercover agents during wartime.

SUTLER   A civilian who followed the army in order to sell sweets, alcohol, and other luxury items to soldiers.

UNION   Also known as the North, the Union was made up of the 23 states and 6 territories that stayed under the authority of the federal government in Washington, D.C., during the Civil War.

VIVANDIÈRE Also known as "daughters of the regiment," vivandières originally served as regimental mascots; most were dismissed or left voluntarily when the fighting intensified, and those who stayed usually served as battlefield nurses for their regiments.

Bibliography

Attie, Jeanie. *Patriotic Toil: Northern Women and the American Civil War*. Ithaca, NY: Cornell University Press, 1998.

Blanton, DeAnne and Lauren M. Cook. *They Fought Like Demons: Women Soldiers in the American Civil War*. Baton Rouge, LA: Louisiana State University, 2002.

Burgess, Lauren Cook, ed. *An Uncommon Soldier: The Civil War Letters of Sarah Rosetta Wakeman, alias Private Lyons Wakeman*. New York, NY: Oxford University Press, 1994.

Clinton, Catherine. *Tara Revisited: Women, War, & the Plantation Legend*. New York, NY: Abbeville Press, 1995.

Culpepper, Marilyn Mayer. *Trials and Triumphs: The Women of the American Civil War*. East Lansing, MI: Michigan State University Press, 1992.

Edwards, Laura F. *Scarlett Doesn't Live Here Anymore: Southern Women in the Civil War Era*. Urbana, IL: University of Illinois Press, 2000.

Faust, Drew Gilpin. *Mothers of Invention: Women of the Slaveholding South in the American Civil War*. Chapel Hill, NC: University of North Carolina Press, 1996.

Fleischner, Jennifer. *Mrs. Lincoln and Mrs. Keckly: The Remarkable Story of the Friendship Between a First Lady and a Former Slave*. New York, NY: Broadway, 2003.

Forbes, Ella. *African American Women During the Civil War*. New York, NY: Garland, 1998.

Frankel, Noralee. *Freedom's Women: Black Women and Families in Civil War Era Mississippi*. Bloomington, IN: Indiana University Press, 1999.

Gansler, Laura Leedy. *The Mysterious Private Thompson: The Double Life of Sarah Emma Edmonds, Civil War Soldier*. New York, NY: Free Press, 2005.

Garrison, Nancy Scripture. *With Courage and Delicacy: Civil War on the Peninsula: Women and the U.S. Sanitary Commission*. Mason City, IA: Savas, 1999.

Hall, Larry. "Civil War-Era Women Used Charm as Means to an End." *Richmond Times-Dispatch*, March 3, 2004.

Hall, Richard H. *Patriots in Disguise: Women Warriors of the Civil War Era*. New York, NY: Paragon House, 1993.

Hall, Richard H. *Women on the Civil War Battlefront*. Lawrence, KS: University Press of Kansas, 2006.

Jones, Bessie Z., ed. *Hospital Sketches by Louisa May Alcott*. Cambridge, MA.: Harvard University Press, 1960.

Leonard, Elizabeth D. *All the Daring of the Soldier: Women of the Civil War Armies*. New York, NY: W.W. Norton, 1999.

Lowry, Thomas P. *Confederate Heroines: 120 Southern Women Convicted by Union Military Justice*. Baton Rouge, LA: Louisiana State University Press, 2006.

Massey, Mary Elizabeth. *Women in the Civil War*. Lincoln, NE: University of Nebraska Press, 1966.

Mescher, Virginia. " 'Under the Canopy of Heaven': Military Laundresses in the Civil War." In *The Journal of Women's Civil War History: From the Home Front to the Front Lines: Accounts of the Sacrifice, Achievement, and Service of American Women, 1861–1865*, edited by Eileen Conklin. Gettysburg, PA: Thomas Publications, 2001.

Moore, Frank, ed. *The Rebellion Record: A Diary of American Events*. New York, NY: Putnam, 1863.

Nelson, Scott Reynolds and Carol Sheriff. *A People at War: Civilians and Soldiers in America's Civil War, 1854–1877*. New York, NY: Oxford University Press, 2008.

Pember, Phoebe Yates. *A Southern Woman's Story: Life in Confederate Richmond, Including Unpublished Letters Written from the Chimborazo Hospital*. Wilmington, NC: Broadfoot Publishing, 1991.

Schultz, Jane E. *Women at the Front: Hospital Workers in Civil War America*. Chapel Hill, NC: University of North Carolina Press, 2004.

Silber, Nina. *Daughters of the Union: Northern Women Fight the Civil War*. Cambridge, MA: Harvard University Press, 2005.

Taylor, Kay Ann. "Mary S. Peake and Charlotte L. Forten: Black Teachers During the Civil War and Reconstruction." *The Journal of Negro Education* (Spring 2005): 124–137.

Taylor, Susie King. *A Black Woman's Civil War Memoirs: Reminiscences of My Life in Camp with the 33rd U.S. Colored Troops*. New York, NY: Arno Press, 1978. First published 1902.

Woodward, C. Vann, ed. *Mary Chesnut's Civil War*. New Haven, CT: Yale University Press, 1981.

Youngs, Rosemary. *The Civil War Diary Quilt: 121 Stories and the Quilt Blocks They Inspired*. Iola, WI: Krause Publications, 2005.

Further Resources

Beller, Susan Provost. *Confederate Ladies of Richmond*. Brookfield, CT: Twenty-First Century, 1999.

Caravantes, Peggy. *Petticoat Spies: Six Women Spies of the Civil War*. Greensboro, NC. Morgan Reynolds, 2002.

Currie, Stephen. *Women of the Civil War*. San Diego, CA: Lucent, 2003.

Garrison, Webb. *Amazing Women of the Civil War*. Nashville, TN: Rutledge Hill Press, 1999.

Harper, Judith E., ed. *Women During the Civil War: An Encyclopedia*. New York, NY: Routledge, 2003.

Malone, Margaret Gay. *The Diary of Susie King Taylor, Civil War Nurse*. New York, NY: Benchmark, 2003.

Slavicek, Louise Chipley. *Harriet Tubman and the Underground Railroad*. San Diego, CA: Lucent, 2006.

Zeinert, Karen. *Those Courageous Women of the Civil War*. Brookfield, CT: Millbrook Press, 1998.

WEB SITES

Our Army Nurses
http://www.edinborough.com/Learn/cw_nurses/Nurses.html

Civil War Women: Primary Sources on the Internet
http://library.duke.edu/specialcollections/bingham/guides/cwdocs.html

Civil War Women: Women Were There
http://userpages.aug.com/captbarb/femvets2.html

The Daughter of the Regiment: A Brief History of Vivandières and Cantinières in the American Civil War
http://ehistory.osu.edu/uscw/features/articles/0005/vivandieres.cfm

Dr. Mary Edwards Walker
http://www.thelizlibrary.org/undelete/military/mil3walker.html

Harriet Tubman
http://www.harriettubman.com

Women and the American Civil War
http://womenshistory.about.com/od/civilwar/Women_and_the_
    American_Civil_War.htm

Women of the American Civil War
http://americancivilwar.com/women/women.html

Picture Credits

Index

About the Authors

LOUISE CHIPLEY SLAVICEK received her master's degree in history from the University of Connecticut. She is the author of numerous periodical articles and more than 20 other books for young people on historical topics, including *Women of the American Revolution, Israel,* and *The Great Wall of China.*

TIM MCNEESE is associate professor of history at York College in York, Nebraska, where he is in his seventeenth year of college instruction. Professor McNeese earned an associate of arts degree from York College, a bachelor of arts in history and political science from Harding University, and a master of arts in history from Missouri State University. A prolific author of books for elementary, middle, and high school, and college readers, McNeese has published more than 100 books and educational materials over the past 20 years, on everything from the founding of early New York to Hispanic authors. His writing has earned him a citation in the library reference work *Contemporary Authors*, and multiple citations in *Best Books for Young Teen Readers*. In 2006, McNeese appeared on the History Channel program *Risk Takers, History Makers: John Wesley Powell and the Grand Canyon*. He was a faculty member at the 2006 Tony Hillerman Writers Conference in Albuquerque. His wife, Beverly, is an assistant professor of English at York College. They have two married children, Noah and Summer, and three grandchildren, Ethan, Adrianna, and Finn William. Tim and Bev McNeese sponsored study trips for college students on the Lewis and Clark Trail in 2003 and 2005 and to the American Southwest in 2008. You may contact Professor McNeese at tdmcneese@york.edu.